Acclaim for
LiViNG SEReNDIPITOUSLY

"The message of *Living Serendipitously* is an important one. We can never hear it too many times."
— Renee Welfeld, Author of *Your Body's Wisdom: A Body-Centered Approach to Transformation*

"I was on my way to New York to give an important presentation when I began reading *Living Serendipitously*. I wanted to finish it before the presentation because I knew it would make a big difference — and it did!"
— Miriam Jaskierowicz Arman, Director, International Academy of Voice and Stage
Author of *The Voice: A Spiritual Approach to Singing, Speaking and Communicating*

"I love this book. I've used portions of it for my bereavement support group and at many of my retreats. It's one of those rare books that touches people's hearts and changes their lives."
— Jane Lombardo, Retreat Director, "Outreach to Women"

"It was a most delightful experience for me to read *Living Serendipitously*. I am sure readers will enjoy this facinating book."
— Father Joseph F. Girzone, Author of the *Joshua* books

"Madeleine Kay has, with wit, humor and incredible honesty, written a book that will actually make you happy. It will make you want to dance and sing . . . want to live, laugh and just love your life."
— Hope Christensen, President, Creative Overload Public Relations

"I read *Living Serendipitously* and just loved it. In fact, I have recommended it to everyone in my book club and am recommending it to all my Feng Shui clients. This book says more about the positive use of energy than any Feng Shui book I've ever read."
— Janeen Wynn, Feng Shui Consultant

"The thing I got out of this book is that I'm no longer afraid to take risks. I'm now excited about it. *Living Serendipitously* inspires people not to wait to do what they dream of."

— Theresa Baldwin, Owner, Mountain Country Cupboard Gift Shop

"I loved *Living Serendipitously . . . Keeping the Wonder Alive.* I keep it right beside my bed and pick it up any time I'm feeling bad, and it always makes me feel happy." — Clarence C. Hope III, Horticulture Professor

"*Living Serendipitously* is one of those books you never want to finish. It is such an inspiring book . . . it has filled me with a sense of wonder and excitement. It is a book I will want to read again and again."

— Marjorie A. Houtz, Equestrian

"I can't tell you what this book has meant to me . . . it has made all the difference in my life. Since reading it, I've bought seven more copies to give to my friends and family." — Beth Ellis, Home Schooling Mother of Three

"After reading this book, I felt like I could do anything. The energy of *Living Serendipitously* is tranformative. It helps you live more joyfully and richly right now. In today's times, a book like this is invaluable. I highly recommend it." — Cindy Sealy, Musician

"*Living Serendipitously* is such a provocative book for emotional healing. It is very much of a self-help book that tells it like it is and leaves you with such a positive attitude . . . Wow!" — David Gibson, Computer Technician

LiViNg

SeReNDipiTOUSLY

keeping the
wonder alive

LiViNG

SeRENDipiTOUSLY

keeping the
wonder alive

MADELEINE KAY

Chrysalis Publishing

Copyright © 2003 Madeleine Kay

Published by:
Chrysalis Publishing
PO Box 675
Flat Rock, NC 28731
Tel (828) 692-9840 / Fax (828) 698-8343
www.livingserendipitously.com

Cataloging-in-Publication Data
Kay, Madeleine.
Living serendipitously—keeping the wonder alive / Madeleine Kay.
p. cm.
LCCN 2001119359
ISBN 0-9715572-3-3
1. Self-realization. 2. Conduct of life.
3. Happiness. I. Title.
BJ1470.K39 2003   170'.44
QB133-1151

Printed in the United States of America

First Printing
10 9 8 7 6 5 4 3 2 1

i thank You God for most this amazing
day:for the leaping greenly spirits of trees
and a blue true dream of sky;and for everything
which is natural which is infinite which is yes

E.E. Cummings

ACKNOWLEDGMENTS

First and foremost I would like to thank my Muse, the Force, or God — whoever or whatever wrote this book, for surely it wasn't I.

My parents, Harry and Anne Kay, for being such wonderful people and being my parents . . . my dad, for always telling me I could do anything I want in life, if I want it badly enough — and my mom, for her determination and child-like enthusiasm . . . and most of all, for their respect and unconditional love.

My son, Daniel Sage, for being such a great son, person and friend . . . and my greatest teacher.

My sister, Lorraine Robinson, for being there when I needed, and my brother-in-law Robbie, for reminding me what I learned from my parents about love.

My nieces, Jackie Confrey and Lisa Silver, and my whole wonderful family for always seeing the child in me.

All of my friends who have always believed in and supported me, who have seen the wonder . . . and appreciated it in me: Carole Abril, Wes Burlingame, Courtney and Patty Cauldwell, Hope Christensen, Manuela Cobos, Yves Debarge, Susana Escayola, Marilyn Gasque, David Gibson, Ariel Harris, Claude Kieffer, Lee Liebowitz, Janie Lotierzo, Lesley Reifert, Lisabeth Reynolds, Alyssa Rose, John and Thea Rosmini, Eileen Ross, Cindy Sealy,

ACKNOWLEDGMENTS

Federico Velludo, Haze Wainberg, Claude Zeligman, my walking friends, Rose Deffet and Anna Wong, and all my friends at InterPlay®, especially Meg MacLeod.

All the singers, songwriters, musicians, artists, writers and all the people I have ever met — who have inspired and empowered me . . . and touched my heart.

DAO Master Johnny Mohr, DAO Master Cynthia Fung, Kathleen Bailey and all my friends and relatives at the Rong Deh Temple who gave me a sanctuary when I needed it.

All the healers and alternative care professionals, especially Dr. Shyam Badlani, Dr. Bill Brooks, Dr. Paul Canali, Dr. Herb Dandes, Dr. Marie Andersson-Frees (and Barbara), Linda Gardner, Dr. Frank Trombetta, Akasha, Valerie Heavens, and Bethany Ray, who were always there, like true physicians, whenever I needed.

Kerry Lindsey, for having the same vision I did . . . and building it, so I could return *home* and live how and where I want.

All the wonderful people who helped me get this book out — just as I wanted and when I wanted — especially Yvonne McCall-Dickson, Bill Humleker, John Martz (for the font), Dan Poynter, Linda Smith, the people at Keen Impressions and Cypress House (especially Cynthia Frank and Joe Shaw), and my angel *everything* person, Claire Collins, for her friendship and continuous help and support.

My treasured books: *Siddhartha, Hope for the Flowers* and *Letters to a Young Poet.*

My dog Yoda, for keeping me company during the publication process.

And most of all — to Life — this crazy, wonderful adventure with all its mystery, wonder and surprises. I am eternally grateful to be alive . . . to have the opportunity to see anew every day . . . and to always create something beautiful . . . thank you.

What I think is that being alive is a tremendous opportunity. It's what you do with it that matters.

Katharine Hepburn

There are only two things you can give your children,
and they are roots and wings.

To my father and mother, who gave me
these *portable roots.*

To my good friend, soul-mate and spirit guide,
Thea, who saw them and always knew they
were there, even when I didn't.

And to my son, Daniel, who never let me
forget them and always brings me back to
them.

CONTENTS

Part 1

Chapter

Part 2

I believe in grabbing at Life.
Every minute a new minute.
Every second a new second
. . . never happened before.

Zorba the Greek
Nikos Kazantzakis

Special Dedication

To my father —
Thank you for everything . . .

I love you Daddy

Life is not a problem to be solved, but a mystery to be lived.

Thomas Merton

INTRODUCTION

Why Serendipitously? Why not "The Rapture of Being Alive" or "Living in Wonder" or just — "Happiness" — yes, why not just "Happiness" as a title?

First of all, because I like the way the word just rolls off the tongue — *serendipity** — it has a playful quality to it, and sounds are so important to how we feel.

But more important, because serendipity is an attitude . . . no, not an attitude; that's too cerebral. It is a state . . . no, not that either. A state is too static and serendipity is organic, ALIVE. It is a beingness, an openness, a NOWNESS, (I'm sure that's not a word, but it should be). It is a receptivity to anything and everything, a constant blossoming, a wonderful feeling of anticipation that at any moment, something wonderful is about to happen. And when you live this way, wonderful things do always happen and appear in your life because your expectation brings them into being.

---

* Serendipity is defined as the knack for finding wonderful, unexpected surprises not sought for.

Either by materializing them, or just making you aware of them — kind of like looking at life through rose-colored glasses. Many people denigrate looking at the world this way (which we will get to later), but it's a marvelous, healthy, inspiring way to live your life — and always improves the quality and performance of it . . . and . . . I would venture to say, the longevity as well.

So serendipity is a calling, a willingness to live your life as if everything is a miracle, with the belief that at any moment something wonderful is about to happen. Einstein said there are only two ways to live your life — as though nothing is a miracle or as though everything is a miracle.

The choice is yours. Most people however, do not even realize they have a choice and fall into a pattern of the former. But you do have a choice — and serendipity is the way of beauty, joy, and truth. It is innocence and love being born every moment. Experience it. Don't miss it.

Serendipity is the pulse of life that lets us know we are alive, which as Joseph Campbell says in *The Power of Myth*, is what all of us are seeking — the experience of being alive. Not meaning, not riches, not fame, but the "rapture," the exquisite pain "of being alive." Yes, life is sometimes painful (not nearly as often as most people believe, but we'll get to that later too), but if you live even the pain serendipitously — it is an exquisite pain.

This exquisite pain assaulted me two years ago when I had a nervous breakdown as a result of being in a long-term relationship and in business with someone whose over-powering negative energy was so antithetical to mine, it was devastating to my soul. From the very first moment the breakdown began however, I actually felt a strange excitement, a sense of wonder and anticipation at the new discoveries I was making every moment, the momentous awakening taking place within me every second; at the exquisite heightened sensitivity I felt to everything, so that even the slightest thing made being in the world almost unbearably painful. Yet, this too was exquisite and I found a joy, a richness in it that fed me and nourished me — that gave me the energy I needed to do what I had to do.

For by living even our pain and our sadnesses serendipitously, by giving in to them entirely, we make friends with them, and in this way, are able to learn the lessons we are meant to learn from them. As the German poet Rainer Maria Rilke tells us in his wonderful little book, *Letters to a Young Poet*, "Sickness is the means by which an organism frees itself of foreign matter; so one must just help it to be sick, to have its whole sickness and break out with it, for that is its progress."

"Were it possible for us to see further than our knowledge reaches," he says, "and yet a little way beyond the outworks of our divining, perhaps we would endure our sadnesses with greater confidence than our joys. For they are the moments when something new has entered into us, something unknown; our feelings grow mute in shy perplexity, everything in us withdraws, a stillness comes, and the new, which no one knows, stands in the midst of it and is silent."

So living serendipitously forces you to live in the NOW, to appreciate every glorious, miraculous moment — to notice everything — even the smallest thing — and see its beauty.

Although I had lived serendipitously most of my life, I had never really thought about it, never conceptualized it until I went to Israel thirty-two years ago. There I found an electricity, a vitality, an intense passionate appreciation of . . .

no, not appreciation . . . rather a living of Life. What I call a "sense of immediacy," a hedonism. Oh, not hedonism as I had always thought of it as a rather superficial and frivolous seeking of pleasure, but a genuine, deep, visceral gut reaction to living   *Life in the moment*. This hedonism creates a certain energy and pulse that infuse life with rapture, passion, richness and serenity.

Which brings me to the final reason why *Living Serendipitously* is the title of this book. A reason I discovered amidst the turmoil of two years ago. A reason best expressed by what I wrote only seven days into it:

> At this moment, I feel calm — almost like
> I imagine a butterfly feels when it is going
> into its cocoon for its metamorphosis into
> the beautiful creature it is meant to become.
> I actually feel a serene anticipation at this
> moment of becoming whole again, of recapturing
> my soul, of feeling again the wonder and
> excitement at living that I've missed and that
> was so much a part of my life before.
> Serendipity . . . which for the very first
> time I realize has an affinity with serenity —
> that excitement, wonder and serenity are all
> inextricably linked. I feel good . . .

As I read what I had written, I realized that the serenity one experiences from the life serendipitously lived . . . a life lived with wondrous expectation every moment, is the same peace you achieve through meditation, for your entire life becomes the meditation. So, the serenity is total, complete and all-encompassing. It suffuses every aspect of your being so you are always rich and successful — in the true measure of those words that have nothing to do with fame, money and possessions, but rather with genuine abundance that comes from Love.

Perhaps you wonder, as I did, who am I to write this book, to tell people how to live serendipitously? Why me? Why should people want to read this book that I have written? Is it because I have a Cum Laude BA in English with a self-directed minor in psychology and philosophy and an MA in English? Or is it because I have taught writing at the University of Miami and the University of Tel Aviv? Perhaps it is because I speak four languages, have traveled extensively and have lived in France and Israel, where I taught, modeled and was a recognized published writer.

Surely, it must be because I successfully ran my own advertising and marketing business for years? Or is it because I have been writing my whole life — and the only thing I have ever wanted to do in my life is write.

Perhaps some of these credentials might make some people curious about this book initially, but the real reason I had to write this book and why people will read it, is because I have a gift. And a gift — by its very definition — involves a givingness. It is something to be shared, to be given to others. Like Zarathustra in Friedrich Nietzsche's *Thus Spake Zarathustra*, my soul has become "impatient and full of longing for those whom he loved: because he had still much to give them. For this is hardest of all: to close the open hand out of love, and keep modest as a giver."

If this sounds conceited, it is not. It is a healthy honesty and self-awareness, which are the building blocks of self-discovery — to knowing who we are and how we can contribute to this world, how we can help others. For only by daring to be totally honest with ourselves as well as with others about who we are, without fear of being viewed as conceited or stupid or silly or mad or delusional, can we begin to understand our role in this universe and begin to fulfill it. Only then can we begin to have a real impact — for there is great power in honesty . . . great strength in truth.

Where does this gift come from? From a wonderfully happy childhood full of communication, joy, trust, security, freedom . . . and most of all, love. Where does it come from? Ultimately, from God.

This gift has enabled me to bring joy, beauty and truth to everybody whose life I've touched because of a kind of kinetic positive energy that was so strong by dint of my over-whelming idealism, my beingness, that it just brought sunshine and inspiration into people's lives and changed their lives.

I never really understood the reasons why I had this affect on people — why people in places renowned for anti-semitism embraced me because I was a Jew; why the most difficult places to break into modeling found me working as a model within days; why people in situations where only the worst could be expected always ultimately acted their best; why jobs I was totally unqualified for were always being offered to me; why I was able to enhance people's lives so and why I myself, led "a charmed life."

I thought the reason for all this was what I called my "conscious näiveté" and assumed that since I always expected the best, that's what I got or experienced. But I realize now that not only did I always expect the best, but — and here is the important thing — *it never dawned on me to expect anything other than the best*. It just never entered my mind. Now, we are not talking about an ignorant, uninformed person. I was highly intelligent, well-read, widely traveled, and had delved very deeply into many philosophical subjects by this time. Yet, I still somehow maintained an innocence that was thoroughly pure, honest and intact. And, as *The Course in Miracles* tells us, "Innocence is wisdom. . . . It is perfectly aware of everything that is true."

Then two years ago, I had the nervous breakdown and my wholisitic-oriented way of living was submerged in a detail-oriented, fragmented, scattered mind — and, for the first time in my life, I experienced fear, separateness and worrying — I was overwhelmed by a barrage of "what ifs." As I worked through this process, I understood for the very first time how so many people live most of their lives, and more important, I realized the starting point for many people's actions, motives and behavior. For the very first time, I found that I truly understood other people's fear, pain and the enormous suffering in the world.

Prior to this, despite all my compassion and empathy, I never really understood the depth and breadth of other people's pain, because I thought everyone's starting point was the same as mine — a place of immense security rooted in a blissful freedom; a place of wholeness and unity; a place of love and empathy and non-judgement; a place of innocence, total trust, faith and intuitive knowing; a place of serendipitous expectation of only the best every moment where just the thought and then the action existed with no details, no "what ifs" — only — "sure, why nots."

So I had to lose all this temporarily in order to understand it. For it was always how I had lived intuitively, preconceptually. It was my beingness — and in order to appreciate it and conceptualize it so I could help, teach and show others this "way of being" — I had to first become like everybody else and see my beingness from the outside. I had to become ordinary to realize my uniqueness. I had to discover my commonality — learn that I am just like everybody else — in order to understand my gift. I had to become mired in fearful living, have "my soul stuck in a stuttering inertia," to rediscover what it was that always made me different — which was, I believe, that serendipitous beingness, that for me, encompasses all the other qualities we all strive for — love, faith, truth, beauty, joy, unity, simplicity, invincibility and oneness or wholeness.

So why me? Because I have an entirely new, fresh perspective to offer. My starting point, as I have come to realize, is different from that of so many others. For me, what is normal and natural, what is a state I have been living in almost my entire adult life — this state of bliss, unity and love — is for many others, some abstract ideal to be sought. So I bring to what I write a non-conceptual experience of living; something elemental, pure, visceral.

Realizing this, I literally began spilling over with joy and abundance at this treasure I have discovered within myself that I want . . . no, need to share. Like Zarathustra, I became "like the bee that hath gathered too much honey; I need hands outstretched to take it."

This necessity really became apparent to me one morning shortly after the breakdown, when I had been asking God why I had to lose my beautiful beingness that I loved so; asking what the reason was for all my pain and suffering. That morning, a tall monk in a brown hooded long robe came to me in a vivid dream. He stood over me and in a very clear, distinct, thunderous voice proclaimed, "You must reread Plato's 'Allegory of the Cave.'"

"Oh my God," I exclaimed as I bolted up in bed. "I've got to get to the bookstore!" I dressed and ran over there immediately, and that's when I knew I had to write this book. For like Plato's philosopher king who emerged from the cave of darkness into the light of truth, and then returned again to the cave to help as many others as he could to see the light; I too had to share with others what I have learned . . . what I know.

But concepts don't change lives. Energy does. Energy that translates into action. And words that contain the right energy create the right movement from the dark into the light.

Words suffused with this kind of energy create a visceral, gut reaction. These words bypass the brain and cause the body to respond automatically, like music that causes the body to move and sway automatically, without thought. Even people who have been told or believe they have no rhythm begin to move and sway to music. The response grows out of their body — intuitively, naturally, honestly — and is therefore, good and true and right.

So I ask you to read this book without underlining anything or trying to remember anything that you read, without writing down any quotes. Instead, come to it without seeking of any kind. For often when we seek, our vision becomes myopic and our receptivity to anything other than exactly what we are seeking limited, so we often miss the true treasures lying about on the sides.

So read this book with joy and an open heart like a flower that does not seek out the bee for its honey. It just opens up and receives. Allow the energy of my words to enter you and make you large with life, so you spill over with this energy, so the words don't get stuck in your mind. For like fat that adheres to the artery walls blocking the normal, natural flow of blood; words, ideas and energy not properly processed get stuck in the mind and inhibit the flow of life through you.

A Venetian painter friend of mine once wrote me that "life is only a dream." I didn't understand what he meant at the time. But when I was writing my novel *Face to Face* several years later, I did. I realized that he was saying that there is no goal . . . no prize . . . no IT. The HOW becomes the IT . . . and . . . like the Wizard of OZ . . . a monumental hoax on mankind lost in a labyrinth of whys and whats.

HOW you live your life IS your life. My prayer is that this book helps every one of you to live it serendipitously.

ƧERENDIPITY

Meaning, Origin and Legends

Serendipity is defined as *the faculty of making fortunate discoveries by accident.* Wonder is something that arouses awe.

According to Joseph Campbell, world-renowned mythologist, the word *serendipity* comes from Serendripa, the Sanskrit word for the Isle of Silk, the former name of Ceylon. In his series *The Power of Myth,* Campbell tells us the word comes from a story about a family on its way to Ceylon, that has all these wonderful, unexpected adventures en route.

Other sources say the word *serendipity* was first coined by the Eighteenth Century British writer, Horace Walpole, as a result of his fascination with the ancient Persian fable, "The Three Princes of Serendip." The story is essentially a fairy tale set in the Fifth Century A.D. on the island of Ceylon, which we call Sri Lanka, which was then called Serendip.

The princes were always making discoveries by accident and by sagacity, of things of value that they were not in quest of, thus perpetuating this concept of happy accidents and good things discovered through awareness and sagacity.

Serendipity is therefore commonly defined as "a happy accident," valuable discoveries you make while you are seeking something else entirely.

There are many versions of the tale, but all essentially are about the gift of finding valuable or agreeable things not sought after.

(It is interesting to note that in this tale, the three princes of Serendip are born near the ancient Mountain of Great Serenity).

When the flower opens,
the bees will come.

Kabir

Part 1

*You yourself, as much as anybody
in the entire universe, deserve
your love and appreciation.*

Buddha

Our deepest fear is not that we are inadequate.
Our deepest fear is that we are powerful beyond measure.
It is our light, not our darkness, that most frightens us.
We ask ourselves, Who am I to be brilliant,
* gorgeous, talented, fabulous?*
*Actually, who are you **not** to be?*
You are a child of God. Your playing small
* does not serve the world.*
There's nothing enlightened about shrinking so that
* other people won't feel insecure around you.*
We are all meant to shine,
* as children do.*
We were born to make manifest the glory of God
* that is within us.*
It's not just in some of us;
* it's in everyone.*
And as we let our own light shine, we unconsciously
* give other people permission to do the same.*
As we're liberated from our own fear,
* our presence automatically liberates others.*

A Return to Love
Marianne Williamson

So much is a man worth
as he esteems himself.

Francois Rabelais

Chapter 1

i LiKE MYSELf

Yes . . . *Like.* That is not a typo. I write like rather than love because I believe most of us do love ourselves. If not, we wouldn't always be trying to be happier, richer, freer, healthier than we are. We DO CARE about ourselves.

But I do not believe most of us know HOW to care about ourselves. Many of us do not seem to understand what it means to really care about ourselves and many, I venture to say, do not like themselves — and this is, I believe, the single most essential element for living serendipitously.

Joseph Campbell, in *The Power Of Myth*, (which is a wonderful series, especially the audio cassettes) says, "If you really want to help this world, what you must teach people is how to live in it." Well, the world begins with you. You are the center of your universe. And the world — your world — radiates out from your beingness, your Self. That Self, you must be willing to know totally, and the only way to do this is to always be brutally honest with yourself.

This sounds more intimidating than it is. In fact, it is rather easy and quite liberating once you've accepted the fact that this is me — this is my Self as it exists in the world now — and the only way I can ever grow and be happy, rich (whenever I use this word, I mean rich in character) whole, free and secure (yes, the two do go together) is to be objective about and honest with myself always. It not only serves no purpose to ever be dishonest with yourself, it is counter-productive and always ultimately, destructive or problematic in some way.

By objective, I mean to see yourself as both subject and object — the one observing and the one being observed — as you would anyone else, not for the purpose of judging, but for understanding.

For only in this way can you mold and shape yourself, like a sculptor creating a work of art. It is said that Michelangelo created each of his sculptures out of a single piece of marble, for which he endlessly searched the quarries, carefully selecting each piece. He is reputed to have said that once he found the right piece of marble, all he did was free the form that was already in the marble. All he did was chip and chisel away the excess to reveal the work of art that already existed within. Well, within you is also a unique "form" waiting to be freed and expressed. You are your own work of art being created every day. And the only way to get to your essence, the masterpiece within, is with honesty.

Only by being willing to be honest with yourself always (in a positive, constructive, non-judgemental way) can you be secure and free and rich and full. Only in this way can you become the best *you* you can be, which is really the purpose of your life — is it not?

Only through honesty can you be your own best friend. David Burns, a cognitive therapist tells us in his book *The Feeling Good Handbook,* that we should treat and talk to ourselves as we would our best friend. This seems to me some of the best advice I have ever heard, and because it seems so simple, it sounds trite. But it is not. It is very profound. I will say it again — "Treat yourself as you would your best friend."

Most of us are so harsh with ourselves, far more critical and judgemental of ourselves than of others, especially our friends. We berate ourselves when we make a mistake, call ourselves names we would never dream of calling anyone else, criticize ourselves for being less than perfect when we don't expect perfection from anyone else (for we know it is an unfair expectation), and put ourselves down mercilessly until we become like a runaway stallion, that needs to be lassoed in. The problem is that most of us do not even realize we are runaway stallions and continue in this pattern of self-criticism until the horse is wild and we are out of control.

Anytime you find yourself doing any of these things, stop yourself immediately. Do whatever you have to do to stop. Either picture a big, red stop sign in your mind's eye; or imagine a policeman holding up his hand and blowing his whistle; or just shout out loud at yourself — STOP! Then ask yourself, "What would I say to (and fill in the name of your best friend) in this situation?" And you will be amazed at how much nicer, more nurturing, more helpful you will be — how much more constructive, how your mind will seek solutions and salvos rather than criticism and blame.

By doing this, you break the pattern of self-criticism; you give yourself a chance to step back and see things clearly, objectively, constructively. Like looking at a pointillist painting. When you stand too close, all you see is a bunch of different colored dots. Not only that, but if you continue looking at it while standing so close, it can even make you dizzy, your vision becomes blurred. But when you step back and put some distance between you and the canvas, the dots fall into beautiful and meaningful patterns and you can make sense of it — and appreciate the beauty and uniqueness of the tableau in its entirety.

Being honest with yourself and liking yourself become even easier if you eliminate many of the misconceptions we often live with without even realizing it. Years ago, I wrote an essay called "The Perpetration of Lies." It was about the things we often do not talk about, the things we speak about incompletely, the things we do not bother to think about at all for ourselves. Things we just accept and in accepting, inculcate in ourselves and pass on to our children and other generations. I called these "lies of silence" and "lies of omission."

Well, many of these "lies" that we have accepted often make our lives far more problematic than they need be — make liking ourselves far more difficult than it really is. Many of these "lies" come from words — words we have accepted without thinking about what they really mean. As a matter of fact, I believe words are at the root of many, if not most of people's problems (but that is another book).

We get our words and their real meanings all tangled up, so that like the roots in a mangrove, we can no longer tell where they begin and where they are going. Words like "conceited" and "selfish," for example.

8

Whenever I pass a mirror, I look in and often stop a moment to admire myself if I look good. I compliment myself on my beauty, my hair, my eyes, my skin, my make-up, my bone structure, my body. Oh not because I think I am perfect — for there are days when I don't feel or look beautiful at all and on those days, I do not say anything. And not because I am conceited either. (I don't even really know what that word means). But because I am appreciating my beauty at that moment — or my intelligence, if I write or say something particularly significant or wise; or my graciousness, if I do or say something particularly kind to someone.

And why not? I appreciate these qualities in others. Why not in myself? In fact, when someone gives me a compliment on how I look or what I've said or done, I usually respond with a very effervescent, "Yes, I noticed that too" or "Yes, it does look nice, doesn't it." Again, not because I am being ungracious. Quite the contrary. I am accepting the compliment very graciously — and HONESTLY. There is great power in such honesty — great magnetism and personal power.

And when you truly are able to openly appreciate yourself in this way, then you can really appreciate others too and tell them how wonderful, beautiful, talented, smart they are — without any envy or jealousy.

It seems to me that people do not tell each other enough nice things. Oh, not about their major accomplishments. That, people always compliment others on, almost out of a sense of obligation many times. But the small things.

I will go up to a stranger or a saleslady and tell her what beautiful eyes she has — or a host of a restaurant and tell him he's really very nice to look at (because he was. There was a gentleness about him — the way he moved and looked — and I liked looking at him. He gave me pleasure that day).

A sincere compliment is never an intrusion and never makes you look foolish. It makes you larger in fact — more expansive — and redeposits some of the beauty back to you, sprinkling it over you like angel dust. And these compliments begin with your Self. Not just verbal compliments that you give yourself, but treating yourself well.

What does this mean? It means finding out who you are and nourishing that person — fertilizing that soil. Not once in a while, but every day, every moment — like a flower that needs sunshine, air and water daily. Otherwise, it will wilt.

The Huichol Indians of Mexico, who are the only native people who have maintained their pre-Columbian traditions, believe there is a flower within each one of us, waiting to blossom. But it needs our tender loving care. We need to find out how to make it grow, and then do it.

Which brings me to the whole point of this chapter on liking yourself — and that is the very important difference between selfishness and self-love. Getting back to words again and how our misunderstanding them directly affects the way we live; in this case, how we treat ourselves, how good we are to ourselves.

Most of us are terribly afraid to be thought of or called the "s" word — selfish — so we deny ourselves and don't include ourselves in with the rest of the world — "the others" — to whom we are supposed to be kind, considerate, compassionate and understanding.

I was at a friend's house the other day where a few people meet once a week to discuss metaphysics, and one of the women there said she tries to be a good person. She goes to a nursing home once a week, does other beneficent things for other people, and then she said, "But occasionally, I do something selfish and go to a movie and laugh myself silly."

I was horrified, but not surprised that she thought that taking time for herself and going to the movies and enjoying herself was selfish. Was it the act of going to the movies that was selfish? Or the fact that it might be a movie with no apparent redeeming value — no message to be gotten — that was selfish? Probably both and needless to say, I could not remain silent.

"Why is that selfish?" I asked her. "Why not treat yourself with the same kind consideration and generosity of spirit as you give to others?"

She looked at me very thoughtfully, I could see a light bulb going off in her head. An Epiphany. And she said, "You're right. I never thought of it in that way."

Then I said to her "And what's wrong with going to a movie that seems to have no apparent redeeming value, one that you laugh yourself silly at? That *is* its redeeming value." For laughter is not the superficial, meaningless act many people often think it is. Laughter is one of the best gifts you can give yourself, one of the healthiest things you can do for yourself, as Norman Cousins tells us in his chronicles of how he literally laughed himself back to health; back to life, in fact, after the doctors sent him home from the hospital to die from a debilitating disease they could no longer do anything for.

"Why do you think you can go to the nursing home and do the things you do for other people?" I asked her. "It's because you do things like go to the movies and laugh your head off. That's what fills you up so you can go to the nursing home and do things like that. Otherwise, you would be depleted."

As I continued speaking about self-love and the importance of distinguishing between self-love and selfishness, one of the women at my friend's house asked me, "How can you tell the difference between them? There is such a fine line between the two."

Since I had never really thought about this before, but rather, just lived it, I stopped for a moment to answer her — to help her understand, and myself as well.

Then I replied, "If you approach the difference between them intellectually, there *will* be a fine line between the two. But when you know it and live it viscerally, on a gut level, they are worlds apart." But this really didn't help her understand. So, I thought some more and finally said . . . "There is a givingness to self-love. In selfishness, there is a taking." And it suddenly became clear to everyone at the meeting.

So give freely to yourself — buy yourself flowers, do things for yourself that really nourish you and help you grow, things that really make you feel good — not things that are merely distractions, like shopping, buying new things all the time, running all over to keep busy every second.

I've noticed that people who are being selfish, or people who don't really like themselves, often say, as they squander material things, "I deserve this." This phrase, "I deserve this," is born out of a feeling of separateness — from anger, defiance, lack. A person who likes himself however, has no thought of "I deserve." He just does things for himself, naturally and honestly and kindly and generously as he would for others. For the person who likes himself, there is no separateness between him and others. There is instead a unity, a oneness.

Accumulating possessions is often a distraction from, a substitution for the real things you are craving — the substance of life which is often found in things very small, very simple, and often, very inexpensive (if they cost any money at all).

Which brings me to the second basic element in living serendipitously.

. . . it is better to be happy
for a moment
and be burned up with beauty
than to live a long time
and be bored all the while. . . .

archy and mehitabel
don marquis

Do not postpone joy.

Source Unknown

Chapter 2

JOY IS YOUR RIGHT

Joy is your prerogative. It's your right. (It's even in the Constitution that every individual is entitled to "life, liberty and the pursuit of happiness.") Just by dint of being a human being — being alive. Think about it — If you're not alive, you're dead.

Leo Buscaglia has a wonderful audio cassette called *The Art of Being Fully Human.* On it, he enthuses about the wonder and magic of being alive — the dignity of being a human being.

We need to become aware of this, to be reminded of this every day. For I believe that many people believe that life is supposed to be drudgery — pain, suffering and hard work — and if you are lucky, you may experience a few fleeting moments of joy or pleasure in your life. Like Job, they look upon life as one trial after another to be endured.

But the "Book of Job" is just a parable. It is about achieving self-knowledge, which is the same as knowledge of God, for God is within each of us. It is about arriving at a place of joy and trust and peace within.

I'm not certain where or when this belief that life is hard comes from. Perhaps from ancient times when people spent most of their time surviving, so modern man assumes life was hard. However, the happiest, healthiest, richest people I know are those living simple lives — those who are in tune with nature and her cycles — so their whole lives have a concreteness, a tangibility to them; an immediacy and intimacy for them just because they spend their time on surviving, so there is no separation in their lives. Everything is integrated into a harmonious whole.

I am reminded of a cousin of mine who never married (actually two) and one of my aunts who bemoans their fate and how miserable they are every time I see her. How does she know they're miserable? I wonder. She never sees or talks to them.

She just assumes that since they are not married, therefore they are alone, therefore they are lonely, therefore they are miserable. Seems like illogical logic to me.

Or does this idea that life is supposed to be hard come from our parents and grandparents, many of whom were pioneers or refugees or went through the Depression. They certainly had life more difficult than we, but they also had many joys and pleasures — extended families, many traditions, rituals and more family life than we do today. But when they see the conveniences with which we live today, they remember how hard life was for them and often don't remember the joys, the simple pleasures that we have traded off today for these conveniences. What makes life easy or hard is not the things we have, but how we live, our attitude — the joy with which we live each day.

So, it doesn't really matter where the belief comes from. What does matter is that if you believe it, then it is true for you, for the only truths our mind and body know are what we tell them, what we believe. And not only does it become true for us, but we pass on whatever we believe to our children.

Oh, not that we specifically tell ourselves or our children that life is hard, but it is evident in our attitude, in the way we experience things, in how we react, carry ourselves, our expressions; the way we live. All of this speaks to our psyche and becomes a self-perpetuating cycle of those "lies" of omission and silence I spoke of in the previous chapter — those misconceptions we pass on through the ages, often because we simply do not bother to examine or think about them for ourselves.

Joseph Campbell in *The Power of Myth* relates a story of a man who was at a restaurant with his wife and son sitting at the table next to Campbell's. When their dinners arrived, the son began to eat his meat and potatoes, but not his vegetables. So the father said, "Eat your vegetables." "I don't want them," replied the son. "Eat your vegetables!" the father demanded. "I don't want them," the son repeated. Just as the father was about to "lose it," the mother interceded and said, "Leave him alone. He doesn't have to eat his vegetables if he doesn't want to." And the father, by this time so enraged, the veins in his neck were sticking out and his face was red, declared, "He can't do what he wants in life. Look at me. I'm forty years old and I've never done anything I wanted in my whole life."

How sad, but how common. I don't know about you, but I know I've heard that phrase said so often (to me and to others) "What do you think . . . you can do what you want in life?" Fortunately, I always believed I could. But how devastating for someone who doesn't and hears this over and over.

YES — YOU CAN DO WHAT YOU WANT IN LIFE. THAT IS WHAT LIFE IS FOR.

What do you think . . . that there is some huge cosmic joke? That God decided "I'll put people on earth, but not let them enjoy their lives — not let them do what they want in life?"

Or does the root of the problem lie in the fact that many people are afraid of the "s" word — "selfish" — and believe that if they do what they want, they are being selfish. Yes — I believe that is it — that 7-lettered "four-letter word" that is so powerful and so misunderstood and overused, that people are willing to deny themselves so much just so they won't be called selfish.

Actually, that is really the ultimate act of selfishness, for rather than being a taking from others, it is a denying of or taking from yourself. So in our attempt to be unselfish, we become the most selfish we can possibly be.

My mother, who has always been wonderful, gracious and generous with me, my sister, our children, and everyone who knows her, wanted for years to remodel her kitchen, which was sorely in need of being renovated after twenty-eight years. Living on a fixed, limited income however, she felt it was selfish to do when she could buy presents for and do things for all of us instead. Years passed and the kitchen got worse and worse and genuinely bothered her more and more. Yet, she would not remodel it. Now, making sacrifices and doing things for those you love is certainly admirable, but not always at the expense of doing anything for yourself.

Then, I bought a condominium, which I was able to get very inexpensively because it was in such bad shape and needed to be renovated, which I did. I was not working at the time and my mother was holding the mortgage for me (as she had done on my previous townhouse, when I was working).

Since I had gotten my condo for such a good price because of the condition it was in, I decided to use some of the mortgage money (all of which I did not really need for the mortgage anyway), to fix it up just the way I wanted, even though I wasn't working at the time. My mother however, felt that by doing that, I was being irresponsible and selfish (that is, doing something for myself that seemed totally unnecessary in her eyes). Ultimately, however, it caused her to reassess how important it was to her to update and modernize her kitchen and helped her appreciate the fact that doing something nice for yourself is *not* a selfish act at all; it is, in fact, a very responsible act of self-love and respect.

So, I want to say very clearly, "You *can* do what you want in life." That is what life is for — to become the best *you* you can be, and in order to do this, you must do things for yourself, nourish yourself so you will grow. So you can self-actualize and become rich and full and whole; so you can be joyous.

Which brings me to another misconception many of us have and that is that joy is superficial, shallow. That happiness is not a worthy aspiration — that it lacks substance.

I recently spoke with my cousin's ex-husband who is very intelligent, wealthy (notice I did not say rich) and cosmopolitan and has just remarried. Since he was quite unhappy when I last saw him four years earlier, I told him how glad I was that he was so happy now, to which he replied that he didn't know how happy he was and that besides, he didn't really consider happiness a very worthwhile goal in life.

During my intellectually arrogant teens, I too believed that; and during my years as a "tortured artist," I felt *real* artists could never aspire to happiness. Joy lacked soul, I thought.

Well, I was mistaken. Joy is very profound. It comes from deep within. In "The Joyful Wisdom," Nietzsche describes the attributes of "the highest type" of individual, the "one who surpasses himself." This *superman*, he tells us, requires a healthiness "merrier than all healthiness hitherto." This "discoverer of the ideal" must be a "spirit who plays näively (that is to say involuntarily and from overflowing abundance and power)."

So real joy that comes from knowing and liking yourself and living in the abundance of your beingness, opens you up to the magic and wonder of life — and then, you can really begin to experience the richness and diversity of this thing called Life — this thing called Self. Like a sponge, you become porous and receptive — always filling up with new life and then spilling over, nourishing others with the water of your spirit. Only then can you first begin to live a meaningful life — out of abundance, not lack.

And once you begin living joyously, you will not be able to live any other way. For it becomes a habit — and our habits, just like our words, actions and beliefs give our body messages. So this habit of living joyously not only becomes a mental and emotional habit, but a physical one as well. Our instinct . . . our very first response to life's experiences, like the tropism of a plant that always turns naturally toward the sun . . . becomes one of joy.

Just as the hand, held before the eye,
can hide the tallest mountain,
so can the routine of everyday life
keep us from seeing
the vast radiance and the secret wonders
that fill the world.

Chasidic, 18th Century

How should we be able to forget those ancient myths that are at the beginning of all peoples, the myths about dragons that at the last moment turn into princes; perhaps all the dragons of our lives are princes who are only waiting to see us once beautiful and brave. Perhaps everything terrible is in its deepest being something helpless that wants help from us.

Letters to a Young Poet
Rainer Maria Rilke

Chapter 3

WELCOMiNG THE DRagONS

If you understand this passage from Rilke — not intellectually, but viscerally — it will literally transform your life. For as Rilke tells us "works of art are with nothing so little to be reached as with criticism" (or the intellect, I might add). "Only love can grasp and hold and be just toward them." And you are a work of art. Each and every person is a work of art. And if you approach each person in this way, you will appreciate the holiness of each individual and you will begin to arrive at an understanding of what Rilke is saying.

An understanding with your entire being — an understanding that goes beyond words (for words are mere symbols we use for communicating and expressing things that come from a place much deeper than words can ever go) — and you will be filled with compassion, empathy and true understanding, which will lead you ineluctably to non-judgement.

Non-judgementally is the only way to live in this world and help it and you to prosper and grow; the only way to be truly free and happy and open. Non-judgement is essential for living serendipitously.

Most people however, approach non-judgement as a concept, and the more we approach it this way, the more elusive it becomes.

Even the very sound of it is harsh, almost intimidating — non-judgement. I can hear the thunderous voice of the Old Testament God in it. Awesome. Something that cannot be approached by words or ideas — something "inexpressible, taking place in a realm which no word has ever entered." That's why Christ had to be a living example of it, for explaining non-judgement, advocating non-judgement is useless. It can never be comprehended in that way.

But I believe the person who has come closest to offering a real, gut level understanding of non-judgement in words is Rilke, in the passage I quoted at the beginning of this chapter.

Think back to the fairy tales you were told as a child — tales of menacing, fire-breathing dragons threatening the fair maiden (the fair maiden being anyone, either sex, who is innocent and trusting). All of these fairy tales, these stories of beauty and the beast, end with the fair maiden kissing the dragon only to find that the dragon was not really terrible at all, only something helpless that wanted help from her. In fact, he turns out to be a prince under some evil spell, and all he needed to release him from this spell was the non-judgemental trust, kindness and understanding of the maiden — pure Love or AGAPE, as the Greeks called it.

If you think about it, you will realize that no one purposely hurts another, especially those he loves; no one intentionally decides, "I want to be mean and nasty and destructive," or "I want to hurt my children, my spouse, my parents." No — those people who seem so are only acting out of their own insecurities, their own fears and hurts and misunderstandings — the "evil spells" which they are under.

And as their lives progress and they live with these "evil spells" year after year, the behaviors and attitudes they foster become a habit, a way of life . . . and become attached to who these people are, taking on a life and momentum of their own, like a work of art left exposed so it develops layer upon layer of dirt and debris until it is finally crusted over and unrecognizable.

If you understand this however, then you can choose to work patiently and ever so gently to restore the work of art buried beneath (for each of us is a work of art) — or you can decide that the task is too costly in terms of your own spiritual, emotional and physical health (for they are all interrelated) and choose to go on your way and spend your time and energy elsewhere. But what you feel for the damaged work of art is not anger, but sympathy, sadness and understanding that the original artist did not intend for this to happen.

So, once you truly comprehend this, you will find you can never really hate anyone, be angry or judgemental again. For "evil" will no longer carry any positive value — that is, a value of its own — for you. It will merely be the absence or crusting over of good — which always lies within . . . waiting, longing, yearning to be released.

You will understand that the "evil" person is in more pain than you are, more pain than he could ever cause you — and is crying out for help. And the only way this person knows how to cry out for help is by hurting others because he is acting out of his own hurt — his own "debris," — and according to the laws of nature, as Dr. Wayne Dyer tells us, out of a thing can come only what is inside that thing. Out of an orange, comes orange juice; out of a grape, grape juice; out of a loving person, comes love; out of a bitter, angry person comes resentment and hostility.

So when I broke up two years ago after a sixteen year relationship with my boyfriend, who was such a person living with personal "demons," I forgave him immediately. In fact, I don't know if I was ever really angry at him because I always knew that he was doing the best he could. If he had known any other way to be, he would have been it.

I mention this only to bring up a very important subject — the subject of forgiveness — which is essential for being whole and free and loving and innocent . . . for living serendipitously.

Ideally, you are non-judgemental, and therefore, there is never any need for forgiveness; for where there is non-judgement, there is no blame. Not only is there no blame, but there is no separateness between you and "the other." And without this separateness, when one comes from a place of unity with all things and people, judgement becomes super-fluous and ceases to exist. For you realize we are all in this thing called Life together and are all trying to do the best we can. And if some of us botch it up sometimes, we are not doing it on purpose.

So, I didn't need to forgive my ex-boyfriend because I never judged him. I understood his limitations and felt badly for him that he lived with them.

The one I did blame however, the one I did judge, was angry with and needed to forgive was myself. I kept berating myself for allowing myself to be hurt so, not just emotionally, but spiritually, telling myself I knew better. For we are always infinitely harsher on ourselves, more demanding and more critical, than we are with others.

It was only once I stopped judging myself and gave myself the same understanding that I gave to my ex-boyfriend, that I was able to forgive myself and realize that I did not know any better. If I had, I would have acted differently. I, like my ex-boyfriend, was acting out of my own nature. So, the love, trust, innocence and understanding I gave him was the only way I knew how to be, for that is my beingness, the "orange juice" within me. Once I treated myself with the same kind consideration, generosity of spirit and non-judgemental compassion I gave to my ex-boyfriend, my healing took place rapidly.

For if we see whatever pain or suffering we experience as part of a process, part of the journey of Life (for Life is not a destination, not a goal; it is a daily process, a moment by moment journey), we will not get stuck in any one phase of this process.

All suffering and pain are situational and temporary and the choice is always ours how to respond to it. Meister Eckhart, a Thirteenth Century mystical theologian says, "the fleetest beast to bear you to perfection is suffering." So if you see within whatever suffering or painful situation you experience, an opportunity, nothing will ever be able to devastate you. In fact, you will ultimately find that most, if not all of these painful experiences, become "doorways" or what the Huichol Indians call a "Neirika" to your higher self, to greater opportunities and growth, to fuller and richer living.

When I mentioned the idea that "within every painful situation there is an opportunity to be found" at a weekend retreat I went to two years ago, one of the women there found it very intriguing, but questionable. So she said to me, "You are divorced. Did you look at that as an opportunity when it happened?"

Since I had been divorced for twenty years, I hadn't given it much thought. So I paused, reflected a moment and smiled, "Yes, I did as a matter of fact," I responded.

When I got divorced, I was alone, had no money, no job (I had only one month left of part-time teaching at the University of Miami for which I was paid a net of $392, and after that was unemployed for the next four months and longer, unless enough students signed up for classes in the fall). I had a three-bedroom apartment that cost $300 a month and I had a four-year old son who was going to visit his father for three months during the summer.

At first I thought, "I'd better go look for a job." But then a light bulb went off in my head and I said to myself, "What are you crazy? When are you ever going to get an opportunity like this again?" (Those were my exact words!) "You have no boyfriend, no job, no money AND your son is going to his father's for three months. Who knows if and when he'll ever go there again or for that long? You can look for a job just as easily in September as you can now (it was June)," I told myself.

So, I rented out two of the rooms in my apartment and went to Europe for three months. And here's the clincher — since I visited and stayed with friends in Europe, it actually cost me less to spend the summer there than it did to stay in the States for those three months.

When I told a friend of mine my plans, a gentleman who ran his own very successful insurance agency, he said, "I envy you."

"You envy me!" I exclaimed. "Why? You've got a wife, a successful business and plenty of money. I've got nothing. Why do you envy me?"

"Because," he said, "you are free."

So you see, freedom is not bestowed upon us by external circumstances; freedom comes from within. And this freedom begins with our choices — how we choose to react to the circumstances of our life. I once heard it said that "pain is inevitable; suffering is optional."

In his book, *The Sacred Self*, Dr. Wayne Dyer offers what I think is the clearest, most understandable explanation of how and why suffering serves as an opportunity. He says the reason why pain and suffering not only function as springboards, but are absolutely essential to greater growth, to breaking through to the next of level of our evolution and growth both as individuals and as a planet, is that suffering provides the energy necessary to catapult us to the next level. The analogy he uses is that of a pole vault jumper. The higher the pole is raised, the lower the pole vault jumper crouches. Why? To muster the energy necessary to reach the great height; like a rubber band pulled taut, to give the most spring.

So when you do experience pain and suffering, welcome it. See the lessons it is trying to teach you. Find the opportunities inherent in the experience — for there surely are. Your very pain and suffering become your agents of healing. Like a Lakota Indian sweatlodge, they cleanse and purge you.

Only by accepting your pain, embracing it, knowing it — giving in to it — can you become whole again. Like a virus, which unlike a bacterial infection, cannot be treated by antibiotics, your pain must run its course. Oh, you can do things to help the healing process along — like drinking lots of fluids, getting fresh air, eating properly, taking nutritional supplements and getting lots of sleep. But ultimately, the virus must still run its course before you will get better, and you must simply accept this fact and give yourself over to the process.

The same is true of your pain and suffering. Instead of fighting it, use that time, that energy, that opportunity to learn, to grow, to free yourself from the past and become the best, the happiest *you* you can be.

I used to think freedom meant doing whatever you want. It means knowing who you are, what you are supposed to be doing on this earth, and then simply doing it.

Wild Mind
Natalie Goldberg

You cannot discover new oceans
unless you have the courage
to lose sight of the shore.

Source Unknown

Chapter 4

fREEDOM iS SECURiTY — PORTaBLE ROOTS

Possibility* Thinking . . . no, Possibility Living . . . is freedom. It is a kind of energy, a force that, as Dylan Thomas says, "thru the green fuse drives the flower." A powerful liberating force that recognizes no obstacles, no "what ifs" — only "why nots." A force for which there is no maze to get through or navigate, just a clear, unobstructed vision of what already IS as a *fait accompli* — for the vision becomes the reality. There are no details in between the initial thought and then the reality.

---

* I say possibility rather than positive because positive is an adjective and is merely descriptive. Possibility is a noun. It has substance — is concrete . . . real.

No thought even that "the universe will take care of the details," for if there are no details, there is no need to even think of the universe taking care of them. The kind of freedom I am talking about is preconceptual — or rather — non-conceptual. It just springs from your being spontaneously and naturally when conditions are right.

Real freedom, such as this, emerges from trust and real security, another "s" word that I believe is so incredibly misunderstood and consequently, causes an infinity of problems for people.

What is security? Is it having a good, steady job? A loving family? Good health? A beautiful home, car or whatever?

Unfortunately, most people believe these things do constitute security. That, as my ex-boyfriend always used to tell me, there is a "script" in life, some kind of preordained formula or pattern you must follow in life — be born, grow up, go to college, get married, have children, work hard, watch kids marry, retire and die.

Whoa! Wait just a minute. There is no script. No preset way to live. You are the writer, director and producer of your own life . . . the originator of all the ideas in your own script.

Again, I believe the problem is that most people accept this "script scenario" without ever really challenging it; without ever even realizing they can challenge it. And by accepting it, they silently agree never to journey inside themselves to find out who they really are, what they really want and how they really want to live. They become silent accomplices to this "lie" that is perpetrated; unwitting perpetrators themselves of the "lie."

If security were synonymous with a good job, a steady paycheck, a home, family, car, even good health — it would be as tenuous as a tray of fine china tea cups easily toppled over. If security were contingent upon these externals, it would become merely reactive, subject to the capriciousness of the whims of other people, acts of nature, all things outside ourselves pulling our strings like puppets.

But security and freedom are anything but reactive. They are strong, positive, active forces — firm foundations — what I call "portable roots." Real security and freedom are not tied to any one or several things. They are within you. They stabilize you whenever external circumstances change. You carry them with you everywhere. They serve you in every situation because they are part of your beingness and no one and nothing can take that away from you.

In a *Third Serving of Chicken Soup For the Soul*, Barbara Rogoff, a survivor of child abuse who was convicted of covering up for her father's fraudulent business dealings, writes about "A Taste of Freedom." She was serving time in prison for her conviction. When she was transferred to a new unit called "Renaissance," which means "rebirth," she knew not only that she would be safe (for victims of child abuse rarely feel safe anywhere), but that she was in prison simply because she "had more to learn to be truly reborn," and she was happy (which is a reminder that in every situation is the seed of opportunity. We just need to look for it.)

When the guard asked her why she was so happy, she told him that she was learning that *she* is responsible for creating her own happiness and peace from within herself. She told him what she was discovering about freedom . . . that only after you believe you are free, you will indeed feel and be free.

She had found her freedom, her security — the release from her demons, the "evil spells" she had carried within her since childhood — within the confines of a correctional institution and went on to marry and become a successful writer and respected workshop leader who works with and trains therapists to work with prison inmates and adult survivors of abuse, helping them find hope and move into personal freedom.

Rogoff's discovery reminds me of Victor Frankl who had been in a concentration camp during World War II. When the war was over, he wondered why some people had survived, while others, who outwardly often appeared hardier than the survivors, had not survived. He quoted Nietzsche in his book *Man's Search for Meaning,* saying that, "He who has a why to live, can bear with almost any how."

What does this mean? It means that each individual is free to choose how he reacts to his circumstances. Each individual exercises his personal freedom through the choices he makes and creates his own beingness — and from this — his will to live.

So perhaps that "force" that I said, at the beginning of this chapter, freedom is, is just that — that "will to live" that surmounts everything else. Frankl's philosophy which he developed in the camp and on which his book is based is called Logotherapy (which I believe incidentally, Barbara Rogoff is affiliated with).

In ancient Greek philosophy, logos signifies reason or order; in Christian doctrine, it explains how the divine agent is manifested in the creation, ordering and salvation of the world — what some people call God, others The Force or Universal Energy. It is the organizing principle behind all life assuring us that the world is not chaotic.

And since we are part of this world, we also are not chaotic. We function according to the Laws of Nature. There is a meaning — an order within our being; we are connected to . . . no, not connected to . . . we carry within us something higher than ourselves. Call it God, the Force, the Universal Spirit — whatever you wish, this cosmic energy operates within us just as it does in the rest of the universe. Thus, we are one with all. There is a unity between us and "the world."

This unity, or rather, feeling a lack of this unity, is I believe, at the root of what often prevents people from experiencing freedom and security automatically and naturally. A feeling of separateness — out of which is born fear and aloneness.

This feeling of separateness — this "hole" inside many people — usually comes from childhood problems, so people grow up not knowing anything else, not realizing there is a hole inside them, a void to be filled. They don't know there is any other way to be. But their cellular memory does remember and longs to return to it. That's why, on some unconscious, gut level, people are always seeking a better way, trying to fill that hole — often with distractions and substitutions because they don't understand what they really need to fill it.

How do you satisfy this aching need? How do you fill this void and begin living the oneness with all things — that unity that obliterates all separation between you and "the world?"

Well, if you are lucky, as I was, you have an extraordinarily wonderful childhood — secure, happy, loving, fun — nurturing in every way, so that like those people who don't know any way other than that of separateness, you know no other way than that of unity. You just aren't even aware that there is any other way to think, feel, be or live.

But most people don't have this kind of childhood, so the way of unity must be learned. And by learned, I do not mean intellectually — for like forgiveness, unity cannot be approached with the mind.

To learn it, you often have to be in so much pain that you are literally ripped wide open — releasing all the poisons, toxins, "evil spells" from you — and exposing the void. Only in this way can you be filled up with the love of God, with trust in God and yourself.

My son, who despite all my efforts to inculcate this feeling of oneness, wholeness and unity in him at a young age, did not carry it within. A child of divorce, he was saddled with his own "demons" that he carried within. But the seeds were there always — the seeds of Love and God — and it was only a matter of time and readiness, I knew. Well, a few years ago, he was in such emotional pain, at the lowest point he had ever been — literally turned inside out — and only then did God enter him.

I remember the incident well. In December, he and his girlfriend broke up. For the first time, he was deeply in love, and now that relationship had ended. Then in February, he lost his job under quite unpleasant circumstances. And in June, the new roommate he had found through a friend of mine after he had exhausted all other possibilities, was going to move in and help offset the high cost of his three-bedroom apartment in New York after his two current roommates moved out. Well, this new roommate, who he sincerely liked and trusted, found another apartment just two days before they had to sign the new lease, leaving him high and dry.

Crushed, my son called me. My heart ached for him and I said whatever I could; all the time feeling deep inside me that somehow everything would be OK, but knowing that he was not coming from the same place I was.

"I've got to go now, mom," he finally said. "I'm going to go for a walk." And we hung up.

About an hour later, he called me back, sounding wonderful! Exhilarated! "I went for a walk feeling really depressed," he explained, "thinking, I have no girlfriend, no job, and now, I don't even have a place to live. And suddenly I realized — I'm totally free!"

Tears streamed down my face. Everything I had ever dreamed of for him, everything I had ever hoped to instill in him, I knew he now had. I have never been happier for or prouder of him — and his achievements are numerous and notable.

But this — this was the foundation for his whole life — for his success as a human being, and I knew all else would follow. He had IT now and he would always be fine. Since then, he has those "portable roots," that unshakable solidity — that solid core that supports him through anything.

So, I have witnessed, first-hand, how that void, that lifelong feeling of separateness can be totally dislodged and obliterated and replaced by unity, by God — and with this feeling, come security and real freedom.

This freedom, this security have nothing to do with things, with having, with possessing. In fact, they often come when we have the least.

This is not to say it is "bad" to have a nice home, buy things, have money, etc. If you don't sell your soul to get these things, if you acquire these things because they nourish your soul, they are fine and will serve you well, will truly enhance your life. But if they are merely substitutes for love, or to prove how successful you are, or to fill the void — they will not only not enrich your life, but they will serve as constant, gnawing reminders of what you really want and don't have.

Some people don't accumulate things to avoid looking within. Instead, they run, they go, they do; they are constantly "booked" so they do not have to spend any time alone with themselves — and when they do, they are either sleeping, getting ready to go somewhere, on the phone or busy preparing for something.

A friend of mine did this until she finally broke down, like a car run too long and hard without adequate servicing. Her soul finally rose up in rebellion shouting, "Hey, look at me. Listen to me. I'm here and I'm important. I demand attention. I need quality time." Only once she began to look at and listen to herself, did she find unity and security and freedom within.

Joseph Campbell in *The Power of Myth* recounts the story of the time he was in Japan for a conference on religion. "Another American delegate there, a social philosopher from New York, said to a Shinto priest, 'We've been now to a good many ceremonies and have seen quite a few of your shrines. But I don't get your ideology. I don't get your theology.' The Japanese paused as though in deep thought and then slowly shook his head, 'I think we don't have ideology,' he said. 'We don't have theology. We dance.'"

A friend of mine in France is an organic gardener who has nothing . . . and everything. He is the richest, freest, healthiest, happiest person I know. He is the embodiment of Nietzsche's description of "the highest type." Oh, he has a cassette player, but if he didn't, or it broke, he would sing. If he can't listen to his mediation tapes because of no electricity, he hums, he gardens, he dances.

So freedom and security have nothing to do with externals. Many people think, all they need is enough money and then they will be free. "I've always wanted to climb a mountain," they say. "When I get enough money, I'll do it. When my kids are grown, I'll go back to school. When I get that bonus, I'll buy a piano and learn how to play it."

Leo Buscaglia's reply to that in *The Art of Being Fully Human* is, "You never will. If you're not doing it now, you never will do it." Don't wait for tomorrow to do what you want. DO IT NOW! For now is all there is; Now is all that is real.

Instead of trying so hard all the time to accomplish things, to do this or that, get in synch with the effortless flow of nature, of which you are a part. Deepak Chopra tells us in *The Seven Spiritual Laws of Success* that "Nature's intelligence functions with effortless ease . . . with carefreeness, harmony and love. And when we harness the forces of harmony, joy, and love, we create success and good fortune with effortless ease."

Every morning I go running along the water. When I'm preoccupied or tense, I feel it in the back of my knees, my neck, my wrist, my elbows — I feel the separate, distinct, jerky movements of the different parts of my body involved in this activity of running — jangling like the tin man in *The Wizard of Oz*.

But when I am in harmony with the laws of nature, my movements are one continuous flow. There is no separateness between me and running. There is just running . . . and I become the action — a moving meditation and I am not aware of separate movements, not even conscious of the fact that I am running — almost as if I have been set in motion and I am moving automatically, rhythmically, perfectly.

And when I am doing this, I am perfectly balanced too. I have a tendency to favor the outside of my heels and the inside of my soles, but when I am a moving mediation, I don't do this. I am no longer bow-legged; my legs, feet, back and neck are all in perfect alignment and I literally glide through the air; not even feeling my feet touch the ground. This is oneness — This is unity — This is the same place freedom and security come from.

We have not even to risk the adventure alone,
For the heroes of all time have gone before us.
The labyrinth is thoroughly known.
We have only to follow the thread
    of the hero path.
And where we had thought to find an abomination,
    We shall find a God;
Where we had thought to slay another,
    We shall slay ourselves;
Where we had thought to travel outward,
    We shall come to the center of our own existence;
Where we had thought to be alone,
    We shall be with all the world.

The Power of Myth
Joseph Campbell

Life is either a daring adventure
Or nothing . . .

Helen Keller

Chapter 5

YOU ARE a BEING OF UNLIMITED POSSIBILITIES

We are all of us heroes. Have you ever admired the speed and agility of an athlete, the grace and beauty of a gymnast, and marveled at what they could do? Well, you can too. They are just people like you and me. The difference between them and most people is that they know what they want, and want it badly enough to be willing to do whatever it takes to achieve it, to become it.

When I was growing up, my father always used to tell me, "You can do whatever you want in life, Maddie. You just have to want it badly enough." I didn't really understand what he meant then. I do now.

I understand that we are all of us Gods, all champions. Oh, you may not be a Scott Hamilton or Tiger Woods, but you are uniquely you — no one else in the world is like you — or ever will be. You are a unique work of art in progress.

And you have your own dreams — to direct a film, write the great American novel, climb Mount Everest, raise a family or plant a lovely garden in the midst of chaos. Whatever your dream is, you can make it a reality, for everything starts with a thought, a dream, a possibility. The only difference between a "dream" and a "reality," is that the former is only thought about; the latter is actualized. Eleanor Roosevelt once said "the future belongs to those who believe in the beauty of their dreams."

How do we transform the dream into the reality? First and foremost, by realizing that anything . . . no, *everything* is possible. The German philosopher and playwright Goethe says, "What you can do, or dream you can, begin it. Boldness has genius, power and magic in it." How do we harness this power? By making choices and then acting on those choices.

But many people, even when they do finally make a choice, make negative ones, rather than positive ones. What do I mean? Well, most people know more of what they don't want than what they do want. And even that is vague. So when they do make a choice or a decision, it is often a "moving away from something they do *not* want."

But in order to have our choices support and direct us constructively — in order to become the best *you* you can be, we must make decisions that are a "moving toward something that we *do* want." In order to do this, you must be willing to really get to know yourself, be honest with yourself — and BE SPECIFIC in what you want. Only then can you begin to get it.

So what is the difference between those people who realize their dreams and those who don't? The difference is those who do not realize their dreams only dream of what they want, the ones who live their dreams take action.

Now I want to make very clear here that I am not suggesting that anyone not be a dreamer. On the contrary — BE A DREAMER — Everything starts with a dream. But don't stop with the dream. Go beyond it. Take action. Believe in the dream and then you will live it.

Another reason a select few achieve their dreams and are living serendipitously while most others do not, is that most people wait until a tragedy or some kind of trauma forces them to assess what they really want in life, to look honestly at who and what they are. So only in response to a crisis of some sort do they take action, just to eliminate the excruciating pain (which can be physical, emotional or spiritual) they are in.

Elizabeth Kubler-Ross tells us that the people who scream the loudest on their deathbeds are the ones who have never lived at all. They have been observers of life, not participants.

Why wait for a tragedy or crisis to motivate you? You, like every one of us, is going to die eventually. So you may as well live while you are alive. Really live, not just exist. You do have a choice how to live your life. You can live your life with a fear of dying, so that you never really live at all. Or you can greet life as an adventure and ride the ups and downs as you would a roller coaster at an amusement park. Yes, it's scary, and at times, it takes your breath away. But it's also exhilarating, liberating, exciting.

Another reason many people are not living their dreams is that they think life is just something that happens to them.

Well, it's not, and neither is success. Success doesn't come to you; it is earned. It is a culmination of who and what we are and what we do, the choices we make. Life and success are not passive states that happen to us. They are active. They are the results of the energy we generate, much like a real generator that creates electricity. As Joseph Shein tells us "You are what you take time to become."

The seeds of success and happiness are within you NOW. They have always been within you since the moment you were born. A friend of mine, Thea Patton Rosmini, a practicing metaphysician with extraordinary powers, always used to say to me whenever we would speak of my dreams, "It's not a matter of 'if,' only 'when.'"

Are you going to wait for a tragedy to turn your "if" into a "when?" Are you going to wait for a crisis to make your "when" then, instead of now? Or are you going to say a resounding YES to Life — and make your "when" NOW?

The choice is yours. You are your own genie. Like in the tale of *Aladdin and the Lamp*, the only thing you must do to set your dream in motion is to activate the genie within you, the genie that has been lying dormant like the one in the tale — for years.

The most difficult part is getting started. Taking the first step. That's why athletes, gymnasts, ice skaters all have coaches — to fire them up, to help them focus, to give them the tools they need so they can liberate the genie within them and perform at peak.

Well, if you don't have a personal coach, reach out. There are coaches out there for everyone, if not in the form of a specific person, a family member, friend or mentor, then look to other sources. There are so many potential coaches out there — professional motivators who have written books, recorded tapes, give seminars; so many local organizations where people are so caring and nurturing and openly give you the love, support and encouragement you may need; or look to stories and myths to guide you, to give you strength and direction and role models.

Stories and myths are very powerful and have been through all the ages. There is so much of the eternal in them; that's why they are called "classics." They tell so much — illuminate the dark crevices of our minds and souls by telling us we are not alone — that others throughout the ages have gone before us and are still treading the same difficult, frightening, yet exhilarating paths we are entering.

If you look upon this unknown path, whatever it may be, as an adventure and you as an explorer, you will begin to see, to feel the excitement of this very moment, this process that Rilke calls being "so before all beginning." How wonderful — how thrilling. Whenever I read that, I feel like a newborn colt, whose legs are trembling with new life within them as he wobbles to his feet and takes his first steps.

So — to live serendipitously, you must be willing to take risks; to decide on and make those three wishes so the genie can make your dreams come true. And what are these wishes? Not idle fantasies, but things you want so much, you are willing to put your energy, your time, your heart and soul into them. You are willing to do whatever it takes to set the genie in motion and make things happen. For once the genie is activated with your wishes, with your one-pointed focus, with a wish and desire so strong that you do not want anything else; then there is no doubt whatsoever (just like in the fable) that you will achieve your heart's desire.

And if you realize that there is no such thing as failure, only experiences to learn from, you will actually come to appreciate, if not welcome, occasional setbacks as signposts along the way, guiding you.

Tony Robbins, one of the top motivational speakers who has spent the last fifteen years researching success, tells us that the most successful people are those who have failed over and over and over again. They have failed 70% of the time and succeeded 30%. To inspire my son, I always used to remind him that the year Babe Ruth broke the world record for the most home runs, he also broke the record for the most strike-outs.

So, how do we learn from our experience? Do we have to fail dismally before we succeed? Sometimes. But most of the time — if we keep our eyes and senses wide open and recep- tive, if we remain flexible and willing to see our mistakes along the way (rather than letting them accumulate by avoiding them or covering them up because we are frightened by them or ashamed of them), if we are willing to alter our course along the way as we see these errors, these miscalculations (like a navigator who is always making adjustments in the ship's or plane's course, but always knows just where he is headed), then we will surely arrive and the rewards will be worth it. For without risk, there is no reward, and the rewards are always commensurate with the risk we are willing to take.

Is it scary? Yes. We all experience fear. The real courage however, is to feel the fear and do it anyway. Oh, I am not talking about taking frivolous risks, doing things for which you are unprepared. But risks to achieve what you really want, what you are passionate about, what stirs your soul, risks for what you are willing to work for — absolutely. Go for it!

And a word of advice — whenever you are embarking on something new, something totally unforged for you (which in many ways will seem very unreal for you until you get further into it and it assumes some substance, some concrete reality), do not talk to too many people about it. It is very important during those first very tenuous stages of transforming your dream into reality, to keep control of the energy, to constantly solidify it in your mind and keep it real, tangible, concrete. If you tell too many people about it, you diffuse the energy and scatter the focus.

And it is essential that the people you do tell about it are ONLY those who will believe in it, who will put positive energy into it — people who also believe in the unlimited possibilities of you and Life — and therefore, they will breathe energy into it — like good, clean, pure oxygen — helping to propel it forward, helping it to grow and flourish.

So open the door to the unlimited possibilities that you are — that Life is. And in doing that, you will begin to experience the magical quality of life — the magic that is you. For if you are unlimited possibilities, then you can do anything. . . . Everything is possible. Wow! How serendipitous.

So say a resounding YES to Life — to yourself — to magic and to dreams — for that is where all reality begins. Not only *yes*, but . . . and I feel very strongly about this, in order to fully embrace the infinite possibilities of who we are, we must change the words we use — and in so doing — change our thinking; for everything begins with a thought, usually formulated with words.

So words are very powerful triggers that send messages to our psyche. They can be tools to help you or weapons that debilitate and undermine you. So choose them very carefully and be conscious of the words you use. Not just with others, but with yourself as well.

I truly believe certain words should be eliminated from our vocabulary and replaced with words of possibility.

ELIMINATE	REPLACE WITH
What if	Why not
If	When
Wish	Will
Can't	Can
If only	When
Should	Want
Impossible	Possible
Limited	Unlimited
Someday	Now

I feel so strongly about this, that I do not even like writing these words for you to see, for what we see and read and hear gets imprinted on our psyches. Lawyers know this very well, that's why they will interject things into court that they know will be overruled; that the judge will say, "The jury will disregard this statement." But of course, the jury can't disregard it. The words are out there. The seeds have been planted and will, the attorney hopes, take root in just one of the juror's minds.

So words are very powerful and repetition makes them even more potent. That's why I have tried to write only positive words throughout this book and why I ask you to place a flap over those words that should be eliminated, so that after you have read them the first time, you will see only the positive words — words that are plump and ripe with possibilities — every subsequent time you read this.

Think about the words we hear and use most often. Do you realize how often a toddler hears the words "no," "don't" and "can't?" Now is the time to begin reprogramming yourself. Add your own words and phrases to this list I have given you. And when you do, think of all the limitless possibilities. And choose your words carefully, as carefully as you do your friends, for the words you live with can ultimately be your best friend.

*Reason is an excellent thing but it is nothing
but reason and satisfies only the rational side of
man's nature, while will is a manifestation of the
whole life, that is, of the whole human life
including reason and all the impulses. . . . I want
to live, in order to satisfy all my capacities for
life, not simply my capacity for reasoning . . .
Reason only knows what it has succeeded in learning
(some things it will never learn) and human nature
acts as a whole, with everything that is in it . . .*

Fyodor Dostoyevsky

A foolish consistency is the hobgoblin of little minds.

Ralph Waldo Emerson

Chapter 6

TRUE CONSISTENCY LIES IN PASSION

I begin to wonder if perhaps all, if not most consistencies, are foolish. Consistency is, I believe, one of the most overrated attributes; one of the most overused and misused words in the English language.

As you may have guessed, it is not one of my strong points. But for a good reason. It is, for me, unimportant as a quality that stands alone.

When I was growing up, right up to today, I so often was told, "You're so inconsistent. You never follow through on anything. You have no stick-to-itivness." This aspect of my personality was viewed as a negative by my elders and the statements meant to point out certain "deficiencies" in my character.

Fortunately, I had such a solid center and strong sense of self, that these statements rarely affected me. Oh, momentarily yes — I'd stop and think about it. But ultimately, they never really affected how I've lived my life because I never really felt consistency was very important. It just didn't seem relevant. I was too busy living my life to worry about being consistent.

What is consistency anyway? What is this thing called stick-to-itiveness? When does it start and where does it end? Does it mean that everything you start, you must stick with until . . . until . . . until what? Until when? Until you die? Until it's over for some external reason — like you move, or the place closes, or you retire, or you become rich? Does it mean that you should not ever start anything unless you are going to "stick with it?" And who determines all this anyway?

Where is the room — the latitude, the space — for change, for growth, for evolution? And most important . . . where is the room for experimentation, excitement, discovery?

Doesn't consistency mean doing something as long as it satisfies you? Feeds your soul? Nourishes you? For isn't that ultimately why we do things? Or why we would like to do things, if we didn't get caught up in habits, routines and external things and patterns that have nothing to do with our real life — which is the life we want to live and the one we are meant to live?

Isn't the time to stop doing something once it no longer satisfies us? Satisfies whatever reason we began it for? Once we have grown beyond it and it has served its purpose in our evolutionary process?

Oh, I'm not talking about indiscriminately discarding people or jobs in our lives because of a utilitarianism that finds them no longer useful.

I am speaking of developing and fostering a flexibility and curiosity that enable and encourage us to change, to adapt, to grow. Just like we discard (and hopefully recycle) as we grow, clothes that no longer fit us, toys that no longer stimulate us, we must be willing to shed, like a snake periodically sheds its old skin, those things in our lives that no longer are conducive to our continual growth and development. This is not frivolous — this is the way of nature.

Unfortunately, many of us get stuck in habits and patterns and routines and stay in them long past the time they serve any constructive purpose in our lives. Sometimes, we stay because we are afraid of the unknown. Sometimes because of the "s" word — what we believe is "security" — or the "f" word — "fear." And sometimes we stay because we just never thought of not staying. It's become a habit — something we do by rote and do not even think about or question.

And then some of us stay in old routines because we are afraid people will call us irresponsible, flighty, fickle; afraid people will say we are confused, we don't know what we want, we are all mixed up; afraid people will think we are failures and can't succeed at anything and that's why we change and try so many different things.

Unless, of course, we are wealthy. Then if we try and do a lot of different things, we are called eccentric — and are admired.

But money should not be the criterion here. In the ideal scenario, money has nothing to do with why we try and do different things. Oh, it may be one of the benefits, but need not be the driving force behind our actions.

My whole life, I have done all different things from extensive traveling, living overseas, teaching at the university, learning foreign languages, modeling, running my own advertising and marketing business, writing . . . the list goes on. At any one of these things, I could have been hugely "successful" and "rich" by others' standards, if I had just "stuck with them" to their successful completion. But what and when is that completion? Who decides this arbitrary finishing point?

You do, of course. And that is why, despite what anyone else may have thought, I always felt very rich and successful, despite the fact that I never had much money. And I do believe — no, I know — that most of the people who've known me, also felt I was rich and successful. Those who understood, knew why. Those who didn't understand, felt it but didn't really know why. But success and riches come from what you *are*, not from what you possess.

In fact, the only time in my life I did not feel rich and successful were the five years I spent in business with my ex-boyfriend, when I had more money, more routine, more consistency that I had ever had in my entire life. Nevertheless, I felt poor and a failure.

For I had no passion. I had just empty, meaningless routines day after day after day. But the money was so good, I stayed; just two more years, which grew into just one more year that snowballed into just two more years — "until I have enough," I told myself. But suddenly, for the first time in my life, when I had more money that I had ever had, it just never seemed to be "enough."

I realized finally how so many people spend their lives, how they get caught up in this self-destructive pattern of consistency that parades as "stability" at a very young age and live most of their lives this way, not even knowing there is another way to live — a way according to what author and psychologist James Hillman calls "the soul's code," which is a kind of DNA imprinted on our soul. For each of us is unique and has something special to do in life. We discover this uniqueness by listening to our inner voice, our intuition, rather than by just fitting into a preproscribed pattern and routine — a system — until we are "stripped stumps of identity" and wonder why we are lost . . . why we feel bored, dull and lifeless.

It's because we are not fertilizing our imaginations, giving ourselves room or air to grow in; because we are not cultivating the soil of our soul so we will develop branches, leaves and flowers; because we are not bearing any or enough fruit. There is a reason successful endeavors are called "fruitful." It is because such endeavors carry the seeds of our soul within them. We are giving birth to parts of ourself, born from, within and out of our own nature, according to the laws of nature that govern all things in nature, from which we can learn so much.

We can learn diversity, flexibility, adaptability — learn about just being and about passion. Learn about the laws of your own Self.

One day, I was feeling particularly brittle as I was running. I felt every muscle tense as I ran. It was very breezy that morning and I noticed the trees — their branches gently swaying in the wind — graceful, lithe and flowing effortlessly — and I was reminded to "loosen up," to "let go" . . . to be flexible.

And that is what inconsistency does. It allows you to be flexible — to exercise, no . . . explore your curiosity — that wonderful child-like quality all of us have but often suppress. The freedom of inconsistency encourages us to try things, for if we don't, how will we ever know what we like, what moves us, what stirs our passions? If we don't explore, experiment, constantly try new things, how else will we make new discoveries and open up to the serendipitous life? How will we unleash new passions to awaken our senses and titillate our psyches?

So let your life be a stimulant, not a narcotic. Rather than caffeine or drugs, your very own being, the life you are constantly creating anew each day, can be your stimulant (better than any amphetamine); the greatest high you can ever experience, when you embrace the unknown and plunge into your passions with abandon — with total trust and love.

For there is great power and virtue in passion. It is your true and unwavering inner guide — and like a compass — will direct you to whatever or wherever you need to go. Energy and focus and commitment all come from passion and all else just slips away. All doubt, uncertainty, fear — all obstacles are bulldozed by the sheer force of your passion so that only the possibilities exist.

I am not speaking of frivolous or momentary passion, but rather what Joseph Campbell calls "your bliss." When asked what advice he gives people about how to live their lives, Campbell said he always told his students at Sarah Lawrence College to "Follow your bliss."

So discard from your life the overblown importance of consistency — and welcome passion and inconsistency into your life. Not all passions are grand or lifelong. But that does not diminish their significance or intensity. All passions are important for they establish a way of being, so that living with passion becomes a way of life.

The real passion is to live with beauty — the passion to experience what Leo Buscaglia and Joseph Campbell call the "rapture of being alive." Joseph Campbell tells us that what most people seek in life is not meaning, but "the experience of being alive."

This experience is not found in an empty, formulated consistency. It is found in passion; and in your passion, you will discover your consistency; with passion, you will manifest your dreams into reality . . . and in that, you will become alive.

"How does one become a butterfly?"
she asked pensively.

> *"You must want to fly so much*
> *that you are willing to give*
> *up being a caterpillar."*

"You mean to die?" asked Yellow . . .

> *"Yes and No, . . .*
> *What looks like you will die*
> *but what's really you will still*
> *live. Life is changed, not*
> *taken away . . ."*

> *Hope for the Flowers*
> Trina Paulus

When someone is seeking . . . it happens quite easily that he only sees the thing that he is seeking; that he is unable to find anything, unable to absorb anything, because he is only thinking of the thing he is seeking, because he has a goal. Seeking means: to have a goal; but finding means: to be free, to be receptive, to have no goal.

Siddhartha
Hermann Hesse

Chapter 7

LETTING GO BRINGS ALL THINGS TO YOU

How can letting go bring things to you? Sounds like a paradox.

Very simply — by opening the channel, clearing the way for the things you desire in your life to come to you — AND for the things you do not desire in your life to leave you. So letting go is like a coin — it is two-sided.

One of the metaphysical principles of the laws of the universe is that "what you resist persists." The reason for this is that whatever you focus your attention on, you get.

It doesn't matter if this attention is focused consciously or unconsciously; your attention acts like a magnet attracting into your life that which you dwell on.

Why? How does this work? Because everything in the universe is energy. So the energy you put out into the universe is what comes back to you, kind of like a boomerang.

So, if you are resisting something — something you are afraid of, something you don't like, something you are avoiding — it will only manifest itself more strongly in your life. Your very act of resisting gives it the focus, the energy, the attention needed to bring it into your life, so that a tug of war develops between that which you say you do not want in your life, yet you spend a great deal of your time worrying about, avoiding and wishing it wouldn't happen or exist. Kind of like the game Tug of War we used to play as children — two teams pulling on opposite ends of the rope. The more you pull and resist, the more energy the other team exerts, pulling and resisting you. So your entire attention, all your energy is focused on "war". . . for that is the name of the game.

What happens if everyone on your team suddenly lets go and releases the tension, the resistance? The other team is completely overwhelmed by this release and falls down — and you win the game.

Well, in life, once you "let go" — not only do you win the game and release that which you do not want in your life, but you open the way and clear the channel for that which you do want, like a television antennae that when improperly adjusted, results in static in the reception, but once the antennae is properly aligned and the way is clear for uninterrupted reception, the picture is clear.

Science of Mind, a practical, non-denominational metaphysical philosophy tells us "that we are surrounded by an Infinite Intelligence" (whether you call it God, Universal Energy, Logos, the Force, it doesn't matter) "which operates creatively upon our beliefs. By letting go of destructive beliefs and adopting constructive ones, we cooperate with this Infinite Intelligence in making our lives fulfilling and successful."

From a simple thing like getting rid of ants to selling your house. Now I know, as you read this, you might be skeptical. I don't blame you. I was too when I first heard you can use this Intelligence to get rid of ants. Using this Force, this power for higher things, I never questioned. But getting rid of ants? That's really stretching it, I thought.

But I proved my own skepticism unfounded. When I bought my new apartment and had it renovated, the one thing I wanted my contractor to make certain of was that I was not plagued by ants in my kitchen as some of my friends in the same complex were. Well, of course, because my attention was focused on that, the ants moved right in with me. At first, I was horrified by and obsessed with getting rid of them. I inspected the kitchen for ants every time I walked in there, and found myself walking in there just to check for ants, almost like I was trying to surprise them, or catch them! The problem just got worse.

Then I shifted my attitude. I had just returned from two months in the French countryside, where bugs are as common and accepted as the Provencal Mistral. I sat down and read what I had written in my journal one sunny, wind-swept day as I sat outside my friend's house in St. Remy de Provence, "I am learning to live with bugs. Spiders do not bother me anymore. And all the little nuisance bugs I used to react to, don't anymore either. They are just here. Here in the French countryside, all creatures live together in harmony. It's nice."

So, I decided to live in harmony with my ants and just accept the fact that they were creatures of God, just as I am. And I proceeded to totally forget about them. I no longer bothered to inspect every time I walked into the kitchen. And one day, I suddenly realized, "Hey, my ants are gone." And they have not returned. Needless to say, I was amazed — and am now a firm believer.

I had a similar experience before I left for France. I had my townhouse up for sale and wanted to sell it before I went to France and put my things in storage, so I would be free to stay overseas as long as I wanted. As the time approached for me to leave, I still hadn't sold my house. I began to get nervous, for I did not want to come back from France to that house again. I became uptight, worried, concerned and I'm afraid I was not very nice to my realtor. Finally, I asked him if it was still possible to sell and close on the house in the short time left. "Impossible," he said.

Then, one morning as I was running, the muddled waters of my mind cleared and I realized, "It's O.K. whatever happens. If I sell my house before I leave, then I am meant to stay in France longer; if not, then I am meant to come back here for some reason." Once I realized this, I felt good, and I let go of all the tension, the negative energy I was putting into being afraid I wouldn't sell it in time. Two days later, someone made me an offer on the house and the deal was completed ten days before I left for France.

Coincidence you say . . . I doubt it. There is no such thing as coincidence. There is only that which we set in motion . . . that which we draw to us.

Do you remember that story I told you about my son — when his new roommate found another place just two days before he was supposed to move in and they were to sign the lease? Well, once my son let go and knew everything would be fine, he proceeded to throw, that very evening, a large party he had been planning for several weeks. That night at the party, he met two people whose friends needed an apartment to share — and needed it right away. Coincidence? No, it was the letting go, the opening of the channel, the trust in the Infinite Intelligence that created, no allowed . . . the energy to flow to him of that which he needed and desired.

Normally, our minds are like chatterboxes, cluttering our thoughts and emotions, acting like interference in the smooth flow of energy — of Infinite Intelligence; so that our getting or achieving what we want becomes random and capricious. Like a tossed stone skimming the surface of the water, its movement and points of intersection with the water are random and chaotic . . . have no continuity (which is not the same as consistency. Continuity implies order, progression, is part of an evolutionary, developmental process; while consistency is not necessarily part of an evolutionary process).

Not only is the stone's movement random and irregular, but it muddies the water with its constant motion, like our chatterbox mind muddies the waters of our thought and confuses us — rendering us unable to make a decision or see things clearly.

But once the stone settles on the bottom of the pond and the ripples cease, the water becomes still again — and clear. Similarly, when we let go, our chatterbox mind becomes still and quiet and clear . . . and lets in the voice of God.

Intuition is God in man, revealing to him the Realities of Being. And just as instinct guides the animal, so would intuition guide man, if he would allow it to operate through him.

The Science of Mind
Ernest Holmes

Remember —
The Force will be with you always . . .

Obi-Wan "Ben" Kenobi / *Star Wars*
George Lucas

Chapter 8

INTUITION — THE VOICE OF GOD

The voice of God speaks to us in many ways. Most people experience their intuition as a feeling — what they often refer to as a gut feeling. A native American Indian chief says in the book, *Ancient American Wisdom*, "I always know what to do. My umbelini tells me." His umbelini is his gut feeling . . . this voice of God, his inner guide that is part of the Infinite Intelligence of the universe.

For the world is not chaotic or random. We know that from the laws of physics, one of the most exact sciences in the world. What many people do not know is that both physics and metaphysics say the same thing, just using different terminology. They both arrive at the same conclusion — that

THERE IS AN UNDERLYING ORDER IN THE WORLD
— what the Greeks called Logos, what Native Americans
call Great Spirit, what science fiction calls The Force, what
New Agers call Universal Consciousness or Spirit, what
Science of Mind calls Infinite Intelligence, what religion
calls God.

Throughout the ages from ancient times until this very
moment, great sages, the prophets, great religious leaders and
scientists (Einstein, perhaps the most famous modern
scientist was also a great mystic) have all been saying the
same thing. So the New Age movement toward a universal
consciousness, a oneness of everything in the universe
governed by an organizing principle, a creative force, by laws
of nature — is not something new, but rather a return to the
wisdom of the ages.

As the British poet T.S. Eliot tells us in his poem
"Little Gidding,"

> *And the end of all our exploring*
> *Will be to arrive where we started*
> *And know the place for the first time.*

So this still small voice inside us, this inner guide —
our intuition — is part of that universal creative force or
consciousness. We have only to listen to it to know what to do.

When I was in graduate school studying for my
Master's Degree, I took a course in Hemingway. My
professor spoke about the Hemingway Code — the code by
which all of Hemingway's heroes lived. Very simply, this
code stated that "If it feels good, it's right." Because it was
stated so succinctly and simply, Hemingway's forte, I
mistook it for superficial and simplistic. But it's very

profound, for it is saying that our instincts, our bodies will always tell us what to do.

I had been planning to write this book for over two years. But I was always "going to" write it, just as soon as I figured out the format and which book I wanted to write first. Well, one week in April, I spent a hectic few days and then another few with an old college friend of mine, who is charming and gracious, but lives a rather superficial, busy, wealthy lifestyle. She always had to be busy, occupied, talking or going somewhere. This eventually wore me down, as there was no quiet time, no stillness in which to replenish myself during our whirlwind time together. So, I came down with the flu and was laid up for a week.

On Friday, when it appeared I was over the flu, I decided, "That's it. I am definitely *going to* write my book now, just as soon as I figure out *the details*." Then, because I was feeling so much better, I proceeded to go out, see friends and do things, always with my resolve firmly in place that I was *going to* begin my book.

Well, Saturday morning I woke up with not only a relapse, but this time, I had a sore throat. Confused, I said to my son, "I don't understand why this happened. My psyche is in great shape. I've decided I am going to write the book, so I can't figure out why I got a relapse — *and* a sore throat."

To which he replied, "Well mom, if you really believe what you say you do, that 'Thought is biology,' (which is what Norman Cousins tells us), then why don't you try and figure out what your body is trying to tell you."

Well, I knew what my body was telling me — that until I do what I am meant to do — write this book, communicate, express myself (the throat is the expressive center in the body) — it is not going to leave me alone. But I had already decided I was "going to" write the book, as soon as . . . as soon as . . . as soon as. . . .

The next morning, when I woke up with a sore throat still, I knew I had to do something. I knew my body was talking to me; shouting at me. So I decided to go for a walk to clear my mind, feeling that "as soon as . . ." was some vague time in the future; all the while knowing though that my body would no longer let me live with that vaguery. Then, while walking — spontaneously — with no conscious thought or planning on my part, the title and entire introduction to this book came to me. When I returned from my walk, I frantically scribbled down the notes of all the thoughts swirling in my mind, then wrote it all out in a creative frenzy. As I was writing, I realized, "Wow — my sore throat is gone!" And so was the flu.

So God is talking to us all the time. We just have to listen. Listen with our eyes, our ears, our skin, our gut — listen with our whole being . . . and we will hear. How do we listen this way? Not by being in a state of constant alert, searching for and seeking answers. But by being still and aware, open and receptive.

Like a darkened room that is hooked up to an electrical source, we are connected to the Infinite Intelligence operating in the universe. For many of us, the circuit breakers have been turned off for so long, that we have to first find the fuse box and switch those breakers back on. Then, although the room is still dark, at least the main channel is open and illumination is now possible. Now, all we need to do is turn on the light switch to dispel the darkness with light so we can find our way.

"Most people learn to know only a corner of their room," the German poet Rilke tells us, "a place by the window, a strip of floor on which they walk up and down." That's because so many of us don't know where the fuse box is so we can turn on the circuit breakers . . . We don't know where the light switch is, so we remain in a darkened room, crouching by the door or the window, where we feel safe and perhaps can catch an occasional glimpse of light through a crack in the door or a dirtied window pane.

Many people do not know the incredible power that is within them — the electricity that runs through them — so they reside in darkness and live dull, boring, unfulfilled lives. Not only will being connected with the light source open them up to their intuition — the voice of God within them and all around them — but it can electrify them — ignite their passion — like a bolt of lightning sets what it strikes on fire.

So, how do you develop this intuition? Well, you begin with small things. And as you develop trust in your intuition, you automatically, because you are energized and fired up by the discovery and use of this enormous power you have, begin to open up to it more and more, trust it more and more for bigger and more important things . . . until eventually, you can't imagine living without this dialogue with God . . . without this conversation between you and your intuition.

For example, while I was writing this book, I was quite isolated. So, I began attending a writing class (the first one ever) one evening a week. Totally depleted and exhausted one week, after the first six full intensive days of non-stop writing on the book, I just couldn't drag myself to class, which was held twenty-five miles from where I live, 7:30 at night. Ugh! But some inner voice told me, "You need to go tonight. Not for the writing. For something else." So, I went — and I came back so recharged and so energized (not by the writing, but by the energy of some new people who

81

were there that night, people who were so open, so honest, so real) and I was able to continue writing for the rest of the week, which I do not believe I otherwise would have been able to do.

A fluke? I doubt it, for as listening to your intuition becomes a habit, you find its presence in almost everything you do.

Because I had been so isolated and involved with cerebral activities, I wanted to do something physical, something outdoors, with people and plants, about which I know nothing, but wanted to learn. So, I decided to volunteer one day a week at the Fairchild Tropical Gardens in Miami.

When I went for my interview, I found out I had a choice of two opportunities — one was working with a large group of people outdoors in the Gardens themselves, which are lush and beautiful and so serene that the moment I entered them that day, I felt my entire energy level change, my entire nervous system slow down, relax, become quiet and still. It sounded wonderful . . . just what I wanted.

But a voice inside me told me to go to the nursery, one mile away and see the manager there about volunteering. The nursery was isolated. I'd be working with a small group of people in sparse greenhouses; not in lush, serene gardens. Why was I even considering this? Then I found out what I was doing there. The manager came in and we spoke. Not only was he willing to take me under his tutelage and teach me about plants, but he was a former computer programmer who said he would be glad to help me set up and get a computer system operational so I could transfer this manuscript (which I had been writing long-hand) onto a computer — a dilemma I had been stymied over for weeks.

So you see, the voice of God is not limited. Very often our intuition guides us to something we need that may not even be the reason we thought we originally went somewhere or did something for. But we must be open and receptive and willing and able to read and understand the signs our intuition sends us — the language God chooses to speak to us in.

Sometimes this intuition comes just like a bolt of lightning. No warning. No preparation. Just the thought. And this thought is so strong, so certain, that there are no "ifs," no questions, no details — just the thought and then the action — without any regard at all for how large or serious the situation is. You just know and just do it.

This happened to me back in the mid 70's when my son was five years old. He was in the hospital for the tenth time and sick for the gazillionth time in five years, during which he was constantly on antibiotics and in hospitals with serious ailments. Well, during this hospital stay, he was critically ill, over-medicated and carelessly treated. Specialists were called in and I was told he was a very sick child who had to be on constant medication for many years to come.

I have no idea how the thought or the action came to me, for it was not a cerebral process I went through. It was something else. As soon as my son was well enough to leave the hospital, I took him off all medication and found a chiropractor (something I had never done before and knew nothing about) who did only the upper cervical method (which I had never even heard of before and didn't know what it was) and who used herbs (which no one was doing then — this was 1975!) and took my son to him — and for two years, my son was not sick a day and has continued to be healthy since.

How did I know to go to a chiropractor? (At the time, chiropractors were still considered "quacks" and charlatans). I don't know. No one was going to chiropractors then except for back problems, which my son did not have. How was I able to trust the herbal and upper cervical treatments? I don't know. It just never once dawned on me not to. There was absolutely no question in my mind, despite the fact that everyone told me I was crazy.

How did I find this doctor? Again, I have no idea. I just acted on pure instinct, intuition. And don't forget we are talking about my son's life. He was, I was told, an acutely and seriously ill child who absolutely needed constant medical attention and medication.

Nevertheless, there was never any hesitation, any doubt in my mind. Just the thought — and then the action. It was what I call an "unknowing knowing" . . . which I now understand is pure intuition — the voice of God.

And this voice is in all of us, for we are all Godlike. We all have the seeds of God within us.

The Nike Corporation, for years, had a wonderfully effective advertising campaign — simple, yet very profound. The ad simply said, "Just Do It!" Don't ponder. Don't question. Don't hesitate or procrastinate. When you know — Just Do It!

For several months before I began writing this book, I began to get restless, anxious, bogged down in ponderous questions. "When am I going to write my book?" I kept asking myself. "What format will I use?" for there were so many things I wanted to say and ways in which I wanted to say them. The more I ruminated, the more confused I got and the more "stuck" I became.

One day, while running again, everything cleared for me and a voice said to me, "Do not worry. When the book is ready to be written, it will be written," for the ideas in a book, just like a plant, need to be seeded, watered, given light and air to breathe and grow and germinate according to their own natural timetable. Then the voice added, "And when you do write the book, you will write it in twenty-one days." Once I heard the voice of God tell me that, I trusted it and just let go of all my anxiety and concern over it. I knew it was no longer a matter of "if," only "when" it would be done.

Now, any of you who has ever written a book knows what an agonizing process writing a book is — a labor of love, but nonetheless, a labor. And you know how amazingly short twenty-one days is.

But I had been reading *Thus Spake Zarathustra* and in the prologue, Neitzsche's sister writes that he wrote each of the three sections in ten days.

Now this is not to say that careful planning and thought did not go into this book. On the contrary, I had been composting and gestating this book with intense concentration for two years, like a child that is born after growing in the mother's womb for nine months. When it is finally born, it is already fully formed. It comes into this world with two hands, two eyes, a nose, a mouth and everything in place. That is what happened with this book. And that is why I was able to write it, or rather, how it wrote itself in twenty-one days.

Natalie Goldberg, perhaps the best creative writing teacher I know of talks about "wild mind" in her book of the same title and in her book *Writing Down the Bones*. She speaks of writing as a visceral art, a total experience and says that only by bypassing our censorial mind, only by getting beyond thinking to that place of pure expression, pure knowing within us (by getting in touch with our intuition —

that voice of God) can we really begin to open up to and tap into our creativity honestly.

Well, every activity can be creative, not just writing or painting or composing. In fact, living serendipitously is the most creative act of all because out of that, all other creative acts will grow because every day you are giving birth to a new human being — you.

Follow your dreams, transform your life,
take the path that leads to God. Perform
your miracles. Cure. Make prophesies.
Listen to your guardian angel. Transform
yourself. Be a warrior, and be happy as
you wage the good fight. Take risks.

By the River Piedra I Sat Down and Wept
Paulo Coelho

People are usually as happy as
they make up their minds to be . . .

Abraham Lincoln

Chapter 9

Happiness is a Choice

The choice is yours what kind of human being you want to give birth to, what kind of life you want to live.

How many of you wake up in the morning and say, "Good morning," to whomever you are living with — or to yourself, if you are living alone, as I am now? How many say, "Have a Great Day!" or "What a wonderful day today is," or "It's Monday. Wow! The beginning of a whole new week!"

When my son was growing up, I used to leave notes for him all over the house — on the fridge, the kitchen table, even sticking those little yellow post-ems up on the bathroom mirror and on top of the toilet seat so he would see them as soon as he woke up. They said:

GOOD MORNING DANNY! I LOVE YOU
Mom

or just:

HAVE A GREAT DAY!
Me

Once he got older and stayed out later than I stayed up, I would write notes on large sheets of paper (for now they had to be bigger to catch his attention, so distracted by and absorbed in his adolescence) on the floor of the entrance to our townhouse, so he would see them as soon as he walked in.

HI DANNY —
HOPE YOU HAD A GREAT TIME!
PLEASANT DREAMS.
Love,
Mom

These notes were not only a source of great happiness to him and me throughout his childhood, but when I moved recently, I took some of those "happy notes" with me and they are now hanging up — for me — in my apartment. Happy reminders to greet each day with a smile.

These little rituals we create for ourselves — the habits we develop, can add or detract a great deal from our day-to-day living and our mood. So choose your habits carefully and develop those that enhance your life.

I live alone, with a great deal of silence and solitude, so I have all kinds of beautiful cards, happy reminders and photographs all over my place. And I always keep a fresh sunflower on my dining room table. Like a bright, innocent smiley face turned up toward the sun, it tells me, as soon as I see it, to have a happy day and makes me smile.

All these little rituals and habits are very significant. They are all celebrations of life and job — and serve to make you feel happy and good.

Richard Bach in his book *Illusions* says that people will not understand and think we are crazy if we laugh on the way to our death. Although this is an odd way to put it, it is very profound. For from the moment you are born, you are beginning to die —and your entire life is what he calls, "the way to death." Most people walk this road, this path very seriously, very somberly as if life is a death sentence, so they must not be too joyous. People hesitate to laugh too much, to smile without a "good reason." In fact, they often feel foolish if they "smile too much," or smile without "a good reason to smile."

I find this truly amazing — for the best reason of all to smile is the very fact that you are alive.

When you walk down the street, do you smile? When you go running, skating or driving, do you smile? Why not? Are you afraid people will look at you if you are smiling? Why should people look any more curiously at you if you smile than if you don't? Why is it that people feel more comfortable going through the day's activities with a furrowed brow, or a tense, serious face, rather than with a smile? Why does it somehow seem more acceptable, more dignified, more "normal" to walk around with a serious face than with a smile? Why do we feel foolish if we smile without a "good" and "obvious" reason for smiling?

Think about this and you will realize how incredible it is that almost all of us are conditioned to feel and react in this way. Because of this conditioning, we develop the habit of not smiling. And when we don't smile much, we don't feel happy very often.

But smiling is a habit, one we can cultivate. I have a friend who is in a very unhappy marriage. I recently spent some time with her and was amazed to see how young, vivacious, happy and beautiful she looked and acted. Then I noticed that she was smiling most of the time. I realized that her frequent smiling and laughter were a conscious choice on her part, an attribute that she had cultivated, that had now become habit. She smiled so much, that her body and psyche did not even know how unhappy she was — and therefore, she wasn't.

Norman Cousins — who is the originator of "laughter as therapy" — discovered through his own serious illness, that laughter is enormously beneficial, not only to our psyche, but to our entire well-being. For laughing relaxes the body, improves circulation, reduces stress and releases certain chemicals within the body that enhance the immune system and all physiological functions.

Cousins was suffering from a very painful, critical disease that the doctors said they could do nothing more for. He was sent home from the hospital, basically to die. He proceeded to check himself into a hotel room, rented all the Marx Brothers films and *Candid Camera* videos he could find, and literally, laughed himself back to health, happiness and a pain-free life.

A pioneer of laughter therapy, which was subsequently initiated in over fifty percent of the hospitals in Japan at the time, Norman Cousins spent the rest of his life writing about and speaking on how important positive thinking, specifically, happiness, smiling and laughter are to one's health and well-being.

You see, our body knows only what we tell it. It does not distinguish between a fantasy, a habit, or a conscious choice. It just responds to whatever it is told. The classic case is a "wet dream" or the sexual fantasies of a young boy, or a grown man, for that matter. The wet dream is the body's response to what the mind, what the imagination is telling it and the body reacts as if the imagined sexual experience is really happening.

The same is true with stress or fear. If we see a stranger coming toward us down a dark, deserted street and we believe we are in danger, the natural mechanism of the body will produce adrenaline with all its side effects — rapid heartbeat, pulse, breathing; increased strength and agility. It doesn't matter if the man actually intends to harm us or not. If we believe he does, it is real for us and we experience all the symptoms of the fear of an impending attack, since our body does not know the difference between the real and the imagined threat. As Norman Cousins says, "Belief becomes biology."

Well, the same is true for happy and healthy responses. If we send our body messages of health and happiness by our attitudes and our actions, by smiling and laughing, then our body will respond as if we are genuinely happy and healthy. Anthony Robbins, one of the most effective motivational speakers in the world today, suggests that we look in the mirror at least once or twice every day for ten minutes and smile from ear to ear or laugh without stop. At first, you will feel foolish and have to force it, but soon, you will begin to feel the positive and beneficial changes in your body and your psyche and realize that laughing and smiling are habits you can cultivate.

So it is very important to develop the habit of happiness. Of smiling, laughing and playing. Yes . . . playing and having fun. Those things, those activities have real positive value for our lives.

Many people think having fun is a luxury, that playing is only for kids — that laughing a lot is frivolous and superficial. But they are not. They are very essential to your well-being, to creating a balance in your life . . . to cultivating your happiness.

So many of us get caught up in the minutiae of life, making ourselves busy with and getting stressed out about the unimportant things of life. We forget to live, to enjoy, to be happy . . . Somehow that becomes unimportant, a mere indulgence. We fill our leisure time with running around doing all sorts of insignificant "errands" that we have convinced ourselves have to get done — now — so that we have no time to go bike riding; or go to the park; or sit under the walnut tree in our backyard with our feet up on the table, reading a book or listening to a bluejay sing. Oh no — that's "wasting time" we think. How — when and why —I wonder, did we ever come to believe that?

I remember years ago, when I was in college and had just returned from my first trip to Europe, where I saw, experienced and learned first-hand the positive value Europeans place on relaxation and leisure as activities in themselves. Leisure for them was not "down time" as Americans refer to it (even the name implies something negative) — time that needs to be filled. For Europeans, leisure is its own reason for being. When you are relaxing, you are doing something, engaged in something that has positive value in and of itself.

I remember lying on my bed in my dormitory room, just relaxing — not reading, not listening to music, not "doing" anything obvious to the outside observer. A girl from down the hall came into my room and saw me there. She stood in the doorway for a moment watching and then finally asked, "What are you doing?" And I said, "Relaxing." She was puzzled. "But you're not doing anything. You're not reading or listening to music. You're not doing anything except just lying there staring at the ceiling." "I am doing something," I said. "I'm relaxing." She shrugged her shoulders, stood there a moment longer, then left, and told everyone, "Madeleine is weird."

Happiness also eludes us sometimes because we often become so locked into our lack of positive habits, or more often, our negative habits of anger, victimization, sorrow and suffering that we become like a runaway locomotive — unless we crash into a mountainside or someone gently pulls the throttle so we can stop and regain control. I once read a quote that said, "If you continue in the direction you are going, that's exactly where you will wind up." So stop and evaluate where you are headed from time to time, so you can adjust your course when necessary, usually merely by changing your attitude.

Several years ago, my cousin had just begun a new job which she did not like at all. Then when another new girl started, much younger, prettier and more outgoing than my cousin, her dislike turned to intense dislike and she dreaded going to work every day. The job was boring, the people were awful, everyone was snide or petty and out to get her, and the place was just generally depressing. There was no talking to her about it either. It was just unbearable and demoralizing and that was that.

Finally, one day, her husband could not take it any longer and spoke with her about it. I don't know what he said to her, but when I called two weeks later and asked how her job was, she replied, "Actually, quite nice. Everyone is really nice and helpful and I actually enjoy going into work now. And the new girl is really nice too. In fact," she added, "I think we are going to start a small business together."

Needless to say, I was flabbergasted. "Wow! What happened to change everything?" I asked her.

"Oh, I don't know. I changed my attitude, I guess," she said, "and everything changed."

Another thing that often makes happiness so elusive is that many people think happiness is comparative. I once read a quote by Montesquieu that I never forgot. He wrote, "If only we wished to be happy, that could be easily accomplished; but we always wish to be happier than other people, and we always think others are happier than they really are." Your happiness is not measured by how happy others are; it is self-contained.

And your happiness, despite what many people think, has nothing to do with externals, with things we acquire from outside us. Most people believe happiness is something that comes to them because of something they do or have or experience or someone they meet. Happiness is not a thing and not a result of anything — it is a state of mind — a way of "living in" the world and of "being" with yourself. It is not something external that comes to us, but something internal that we bring to everything we do.

Because happiness is often so misunderstood and so elusive, we frequently do not even recognize it when we do experience it. The instructor at a writing class I am taking was telling us that lately, she has been feeling exuberant, energized, a strange buoyancy. Since she had been going through some very difficult and serious personal problems for quite awhile, she was confused, bothered and bewildered at this unusual feeling of lightness. She felt like something was wrong, something was missing (her problems, her anxiety, her fear). She wasn't used to this — this experience of feeling good. She had gotten so used to her suffering that without it, she felt incomplete, abnormal. Then she began to panic, "My God, maybe I'm manic," she thought.

Again, her good feeling was always experienced in relation to her bad feelings — in this case, as a pendulum reaction to them. Then she concluded that she must be reacting with some kind of ecstasy to her prolonged suffering. This feeling, she assumed, had to be abnormal. At some point, she finally realized, "I'm happy. This is what it feels like to be happy." She was just so unaccustomed to experiencing happiness, that it seemed abnormal and frightening to her at first.

Many times, even if we do recognize how happy we are, we find it difficult to accept. At that same writing class, one girl was at a very happy point in her life. Not only was she practically apologetic about it, but she was actually waiting for it to end — kind of like "waiting to exhale." I wonder, why do we find sorrow, pain and suffering so much more acceptable, more real than joy and happiness?

I suppose it's as T.S. Eliot says in his poem *The Wasteland*, that "Humankind cannot bear very much reality," cannot bear many or prolonged moments in, what he calls "the rose garden," — moments of bliss, of being in touch with the Infinite.

I remember when I first started going with my ex-boyfriend. I was so in love with him and so deliriously happy with everything in my life, I kept thinking that nobody had a right to be this happy, that something bad had to happen. And I'm sure my reaction was not an uncommon response to such happiness. Real happiness seems almost unbelievable when we experience it; so extraordinary that we experience it almost as an exquisite pain — in some ways, almost unbearable.

This is not so unusual if you realize that joy, real deep joy, is often born out of great pain. I am sure you've all heard the truism of the sad clown; heard that all great comedy comes from great suffering.

But why should we wait for pain and suffering in our lives to discover how happy we can be? Why wait for calamity to make us feel we have a right to be happy? Happiness is not something you have to earn. It is your birthright. Claim it. Be willing to see what you have and be happy about it.

My father always used to tell me an old Jewish tale about a man who came to the rabbi of his shtetle one day for help.

"Rabbi," he says, "my wife, she is very unhappy. Our house is too small, she complains. We don't have enough room. What should I do Rabbi? I am a man of meager means. I cannot move my family to a larger house. Tell me Rabbi, what should I do?"

Without any hesitation, the Rabbi asks the man if he has any cows.

"Yes," the man replies. "I have three."

"I want you to bring the three cows into the house," the Rabbi says.

"But Rabbi . . ." the man begins.

"Do as I say," the Rabbi tells him, "and come back in a week."

So, the man leaves and does as the Rabbi says. A week later, he is back. "Rabbi, I do not know what to do. My wife, she yells at me that there is too much noise, too many people and things in the house. She wants I should move us out of there. Rabbi, tell me, what should I do?"

So the Rabbi asks him, "Do you have any goats?"

"Yes, I have two," the man replies.

"Good. I want you to bring the two goats into the house."

"Oy!" The man puts his hands on his head and throws his eyes up. "But Rabbi, you don't understand. Already we are too crowded. There is no room . . ."

Once again the Rabbi says, "Do as I say and come back in a week."

So, the man leaves, muttering to himself all the way home, but he does as the Rabbi tells him to.

Another week passes and this time, the man comes to the Rabbi looking like a madman, all disheveled, his hair flying in all directions, his eyes wild, his arms flailing. "Rabbi," he says, "you must help me! My wife, she is ready to throw me out of the house. It is unbearable at home. It is impossible to live this way. Tell me, what do I do?"

"Tell me," the Rabbi says, "do you have any chickens?"

"Yes, but . . ."

"I want you to bring the chickens into the house," the Rabbi says as he bows his head and folds his hands in front of him.

In disbelief, the man shakes his head and says, "Dis, I cannot do Rabbi. My wife, she will . . ."

"Do as I say," the Rabbi says firmly this time, for he sees the man is at his wit's end, "and come back in a week."

Dragging his feet, his arms and face raised to the heavens, the man leaves and does as the Rabbi says.

A week later he returns. He falls to his knees, his hands clasped in supplication, "Rabbi, everything you said I should do, I did. But the situation at home, it is unbearable.

We cannot move, we cannot hear ourselves think even. Please Rabbi, please . . . you must tell me what should I do?"

"I want you to go home and I want you to take the three cows, the two goats, and the chickens out of the house"

"Dis is it? Dis is what I should do?" the man asks in disbelief.

"This is what you should do," the Rabbi replies.

Totally demoralized, the man walks away, his back hunched, his head hung low.

Two days later he returns, smiling, dancing and waving his arms in the air. He runs up to the Rabbi and kisses his hand, "Rabbi, Rabbi, you are a genius! I did exactly what you said I should do. I took the cows, the goats and the chickens all out of the house and now my wife, she is so happy. We have so much room now. Our house, she is so big now. Thank you, Rabbi. Thank you."

And the man dances home — singing all the way. He is happy and so is his wife.

Why, I wonder, do we put ourselves through needless pain and suffering before we allow ourselves to discover and appreciate how happy and blessed we really are?

In the book *Gateway to Life*, we are told, "Man is not what he thinks he is, but is what he thinks." So think happiness — and that is what you will be.

Faith is the substance of things hoped for, the evidence of things not seen.

Hebrews 11:1
New Testament

We should endeavor to stop limiting God.
All things are given to us, but we must
do the taking. God gives in the abstract,
we receive in the concrete.

The Science of Mind
Ernest Holmes

Chapter 10

LiViN9 iN ABuNDƏNCE

I learned about abundance, literally had it acted out before me, when I was still in college and visiting a high school friend of mine who was living in Denver. One day, she and I drove into the mountains surrounding Denver to visit some friends of hers — a young, struggling married couple.

In the middle of singing, playing the piano, eating and just generally having a great time, I noticed their garbage pail in the kitchen and commented on how unusual it was. (Something, which for the life of me, I cannot now imagine noticing, no less commenting on).

Immediately, a "look" passed between the husband and wife, as he said, "We had a huge argument over that pail when I bought it." Looking over at his wife for permission to tell the story, he continued, "We were living hand-to-mouth, counting every penny, and it was really beginning to get to me. One day, I just happened to see this garbage pail in a boutique and fell in love with it. I knew we couldn't afford it, but suddenly, it became the most important thing in the world to me. I just had to have that garbage pail. So, I bought it. Well, Ellen was furious with me when I brought it home."

"We didn't even have money for food," she interjected in her defense.

"She insisted that I return it, but I refused. I absolutely had to have it . . . **We** had to have it. We had been scrimping and saving, counting every penny for so long, that we were becoming "professionally poor," he explained. "I was beginning to feel poor — and getting depressed, and I realized it was really important for me, for us, to do something totally outrageous, to splurge, to treat ourselves to something nice. So, I bought that garbage pail." (It cost $40 by the way, and that was in the early 70's).

In *The Art of Being Fully Human*, Leo Buscaglia says that most of us are denyers of ourselves, martyrs. We save the "good" dishes for company; we decorate our living rooms beautifully and then never think of sitting in them; we go to the supermarket and stand in front of the gourmet shelf dying for a gourmet treat and ask ourselves, "Should I buy it? But it's so expensive," and we walk away empty-handed because we tell ourselves, "We can't afford it," as if money is the only issue or criterion in life.

Well, like that couple outside of Denver, many times, we can't afford NOT to get it. We *need* that treat — for more than just our stomachs. We need it to send our psyches a message — that we *are* rich, that our lives *are* full and abundant, that we *are* worth it. And in this, we can feel good

104

about ourselves and bring that abundance into our lives instead of living in scarcity and poverty and denial.

I have an aunt who is very wealthy, yet she lives spartanly. She spends practically no money at all. In fact, everyone who meets her thinks she is a poor, old woman, and feels sorry for her and tries to save her money however they can.

Well, recently she became terminally ill, and I took her shopping one day for food. We were standing in front of the canned soup section and she asked me to bend down and get her some Campbell's fat-free tomato soup. "I have a coupon for it," she said. So I gave her the soup. She looked at the can, grimaced and said, "I don't like the fat-free. There's no taste to it. Give me the regular soup."

So I put back the can of fat-free and handed her the regular. She looked at it, turned it around in her hand — very seriously considering the matter — and finally said, "Never-mind, I'll take the fat-free. Here, put this back."

I wanted to cry. This woman was dying. She had close to a million dollars . . . Yet, she took the fat-free soup, which she did not enjoy at all, just because she had a coupon, 3 for $2.00, and put back the regular soup which she really liked and which was $.79 each or 3 for $2.37. To save $.37, she deprived herself. Habits!

And these habits begin very early in life. They begin with the messages we get from those around us, messages that we eventually internalize — that we always have to save, be careful and watch it, that we shouldn't expect the best, that we are not worth it or do not deserve the "good stuff." Those messages get conveyed to us in very subtle ways.

A friend of mine was sending some things to her daughter who had just moved to New York and was trying to break into modeling. As she was packing up some linens to send, her mother looked at what she was packing and said, "Don't send her the good stuff. You have some old towels you can send her."

I was horrified. Why shouldn't she send her daughter the "good stuff?" Why doesn't her daughter deserve them? Just because she is young and just starting out? In fact, isn't it even more important at such a formative point in one's life, to be given "the good stuff?"

These are very profound, basic and formative messages being transmitted to our psyches. So it is important to be very aware of this and to make sure we send constructive messages to our psyches — messages that will nourish us, that foster our self-esteem . . . messages that say "I'm worth it. I am special."

It is important to become conscious of how everything we say and do affects how we feel about ourselves and how our children feel about themselves.

A divorced friend of mine had an eight-year-old son who flew to Phoenix to visit his father during the summers. Now, both the father and son loved chocolate pudding. So the father stocked the refrigerator with plenty of chocolate pudding . . . Only he bought two different kinds — one for him (the expensive, creamy delicious Swiss Miss) and one for his son (the cheap, watered-down, generic brand) and specifically told his son not to touch the Swiss Miss, that the others were for him. Now, what kind of message do you think that sent to his son?

So, all it takes is a little awareness to avoid fostering the development of major hang-ups and problems, often lifelong. An awareness of the fact that everything we say and do sends messages to our psyches and our bodies, for the arena of health is not exempt from feeling the benefits of living abundantly.

A friend of mine, a graphic artist, was suffering from RAS (repeated activity syndrome) and for six months, had been wearing a removable splint on her wrist/hand/arm to prevent pain and misuse. Whenever we were together, she kept fidgeting with the splint, but never dared to take it off because she said, "It would just hurt too much."

Well, one day, after attending a conference on Shamanism, she decided to take the splint off, that she wanted to send her body a different message — one of wholeness and health and healing. And to her surprise, once she took it off with that attitude, she often forgot that she wasn't wearing it and just went about doing things normally and was amazed to discover that it didn't hurt her.

The next week however, she had her workman's compensation hearing for which she had been waiting for six months. So, she put the splint back on — and with that, all the old symptoms, pain and disability came back again.

All in her mind, you say? Absolutely not. What does that phrase mean anyway? Everything begins with a thought — but thought is energy and our entire physiology, as the laws of physics tell us, is energy. In fact, the whole universe is made up of energy, of which we are an integral part.

So, the energy that begins with our thought gets communicated to other energy channels and centers in our bodies and gets translated into physical symptoms and conditions. So thinking abundantly creates health as well as wealth. But we must not only think abundantly — we must live abundantly also.

I have not been working for almost two years now and am beginning to run out of the money I have been living on from the sale of my townhouse. It would be very easy for me to begin to buy the generic brand of products I use or to drive to a different gas station to buy less expensive gasoline for my car. God knows, I could certainly use the money I would save.

But something inside me — that spirit that knows that I am rich and live in abundance will not allow me to do that because of the negative messages it would send to my psyche — messages of poverty, scarcity and lack.

Now I am sure others who know my situation think I am squandering money, that I am being irresponsible. But I am not. There are other criteria in life for doing things than money. Not only am I not being irresponsible, I am being very "response"able — responding to a higher power telling me I am rich and that my life is abundant.

Not only is this essential because of the messages we send to the energy field within ourselves, but also because of the messages we send the universe — the energy we put out there into the vast energy field that is the world around us.

There is an ebb and flow in nature, a give and take — a natural movement to and from, into and out of. And if we stop the giving, we also stop the receiving. If we stop the outflow, we dam up the entrance, blocking the energy for the inflow.

However, if we live abundantly — the outflow creates, generates the inflow in one continuous movement. We remain part of the natural process of nature and that which we give out, we always receive back, for we enter into the cycle of nature and become part of the laws of nature, part of its ebb and flow.

And when we live abundantly ourselves, we find it easy, almost a necessity, to give to others as well, for we are constantly overflowing from this abundance. Even when I am not working and am short of money, I always give money to charity; buy and do things for people I love or just those who need something I can give, whether it's a smile, a flower or a compliment.

For giving is not just monetary. Giving is a way of being that comes from abundance, for as Leo Buscaglia tells us, "you can only give that which you have." If you live with a poverty mentality, you can only share your poverty with others. But if you live with a mentality of abundance, you can share that abundance with everyone you meet — what I call a "philanthropy of the soul." So we can all be philanthropists if we are coming from a place of abundance. And when you do come from abundance, the giving is always gracious; there is never any room for negative emotions like envy or jealousy.

We can give in so many important ways that have nothing to do with money, yet create great wealth. My niece has been a "big sister" (which itself is a priceless gift) to a very quiet, shy, almost painfully introverted girl for eight years. Recently, she brought Celeste and her younger sister, Ronnie, home with her for Thanksgiving. Ronnie was very bubbly, energetic, loads of fun and extremely sociable, always the center of attention while Celeste was off talking to the animals in the garden. Even the smallest creature flocked around her, alighting on her hand or arm.

The second day they were there, my sister remarked wistfully, "It would be so nice if Celeste were more extroverted like Ronnie and spent as much time with people as she does with the animals." As I listened to my sister, I heard my own sentiments being echoed and was forced to reassess how I viewed this child.

So I began listening to Celeste, began really looking at her — and suddenly I saw great beauty and dignity in this quiet, unassuming child. I got a glimpse of her uniqueness as I watched her with the animals in the yard, watched how she moved quietly and effortlessly, as though she belonged there with them. I said to her, "Celeste, you have a special gift. You are wonderful with animals. They trust you. Animals generally do not trust people the way they do you. That's a real gift. Do you want to do something or work with animals when you grow up?" I asked her. Suddenly coming alive, she replied, "Maybe. I really like animals."

And I said, "I bet you're going to do something very important with animals when you grow up. I can see you doing something really special."

Well, this child, who up until then felt dimmed by her younger sister's sociability and effervescence, who was kind of skulking around before, now stood tall and took a new pride in being with the animals. It was no longer an escape for her, a moving away from a painful social situation, a negative experience; it was a joy, a moving toward some purpose, some destiny, some fulfillment, a positive experience. She no longer heard everyone saying, "Leave the animals alone already for God sakes!"

I am sure, in that moment, I made a real difference in that girl's life. Only because I was coming from a place of abundance — and this abundance enabled me to appreciate the unique abundance of another. For where there is abundance, there is non-judgement. You see, all of these qualities we have been discussing are interconnected. And once you acquire and begin developing one, you automatically begin to acquire the others.

However, since none of us is perfect, for we are all human, none of us exhibits all of these qualities all of the time. The times that we don't just serve as reminders to us, lessons that we still have more growing to do, more things to learn — and that's nice too. There's more for us to do and learn.

In my writing class last night, the instructor said that this idea of living, creating and giving out of abundance and overflow is a whole new concept for her. Previously she said, she had always given out of lack and was always being sucked dry and depleted.

I thought about this driving home and realized how differently I perceive what she said. I believe all giving, creating and doing are done out of abundance. Unfortunately however, these things are often done out of an abundance of pain and sorrow, or resentment and anger — so that's what overflows. And that's what causes you to get depleted, because the energy source is negative. But if the energy source is positive, it only creates more abundance of good things.

In fact, I was only able to write this book out of an abundant mentality. As I mentioned, I have not been working and have earned no income for the past two years. Am I independently wealthy? No. Does someone else pay my bills? No. I have been living on some money I saved from the business I was in with my ex-boyfriend and on the money from the differential between what I sold my townhouse for and what I paid for my new apartment — money which is about to run out in four months.

If I did not operate from an abundant mentality however, I would be spending my time and energy worrying about money and looking for a job and would never get to do what I really want to do, what I am meant to do, which is write. But because I know I am rich and abundant, I am free to follow my "soul's code" and write this book, knowing that abundant living creates more abundance.

Twenty years ago, when I had just gotten divorced and was teaching part-time at the University of Miami (for which I was paid very little), my parents came to my apartment one evening for dinner. When we sat down, they looked at each other and then at me kind of questioningly, and my father said, "Maddie, we have to ask you something."

"What?" I replied.

"How do you do it?"

"How do I do what?"

"How do you live?" they asked me, totally bewildered. "Mother and I have sat down and tried to figure it out, but for the life of us, we can't figure out how you have enough money to live."

Since I had never really thought about it before, I laughed and shrugged and said, " I don't know . . . I have no idea. I just do."

At that time, I really did not understand. I was not consciously aware of the laws of the universe — I just lived them. You see, if you had written down on paper the money I had going out and the money I had coming in, there was no way I had enough to live on. But, it worked. Somehow, I always had enough . . . which is all I ever wanted.

So, if you live abundantly, you generate abundance in your life. If you give and create from overflow, there you will find your strength and joy and freedom. And in living abundantly, you will find your truth, your center. When you live abundantly, it will always revitalize, renew and replenish you. When you live out of abundance, it enriches your life . . . and one whose life is enriched, is rich.

This is the day that the Lord hath made;
We will rejoice and be glad in it.

Psalm 118
Old Testament

*I am feeling so much Love . . . so
much Gratitude to the universe,
fear has left me . . . like the
petals fallen down from a flower.*

Manuela Cobos

Chapter 11

ACTIVE GRATITUDE IS A WAY OF LIVING

Most people think of gratitude as reactive — a response to something someone does for you or something you receive. But that is too limiting and perhaps why many people don't live with gratitude, but only experience it occasionally.

Gratitude is not reactive. It does not need to wait for someone or something to act upon you to set it in motion. Gratitude is an attitude, a way of living, an active quality in and of itself — gratitude is a natural response to living abundantly. It is an attitude about yourself and your life that is exhibited in everything you do and say.

Many people also believe gratitude is only reserved for large, important things. Well, **IT'S ALL IMPORTANT**. Everything in life is important. There is nothing small or insignificant. It all matters. And how we live our lives — the attitude with which we go through life and experience each day, creates us and our life anew each moment.

As Susan Jeffers tells us in her book *End the Struggle and Dance with Life* . . . LIFE IS HUGE. This concept is not new. Liza Minelli sings the title song in the musical *Cabaret* telling us that "Life is a Cabaret." Auntie Mame tells us "Life is a banquet."

These are all calls for us to wake up. To open our eyes, our ears, our nose — all our senses — and see that life is a smorgasbord there for the taking. It's all there for us to experience and enjoy. So if your life is dull or boring or "thankless," if you are not enjoying your life, perhaps it is because your expectations are too limited. Perhaps you are viewing the smorgasbord called "Life" like a horse with blinders on, so you see only what is placed directly in front of you with no peripheral vision, no integrative thinking, no associative process with the whole world around you.

A lot of people think that life is "supposed to be" lived this way or that way. Well, there is no "supposed to be," only whatever you make it by your actions and decisions — by what you choose to see and partake of on the smorgasbord.

I've heard many people say — "Oh, I'll take whatever I can get," or "I don't expect much from life," or "Oh, I couldn't do that."

Of course you can. You can do anything you want. It's *your* life. So go up to the smorgasbord and sample everything you want, try all different things. Smell them, taste them, touch them, see all the vibrant colors of the plethora of offerings.

Participate in the richness that is Life and the world . . . and be grateful that it is all there. Open your receptors — your senses — so you can receive the beauty and abundance all around you.

Smell the flowers as you pass a tree in blossom; squash a berry in your mouth and luxuriate in the sweetness of the juice that squirts up into the roof of your mouth; watch the graceful, effortless flight of the butterfly. These activities might sound trite and insignificant to you, but they are not at all. For everything you do and feel either feeds or depletes you, so do things that nourish you.

Experience everything you can as fully as you can through your senses. These are your receptors to the outside world — they open you up and bring the world inside you. You can either hear the bulldozers in the background or the gentle trill of the bird's song . . . the choice is yours. And the choice you make determines your mood, your life, who you are and how you live in the world.

When I run around the complex I live in, I marvel at the variegated, rich marine life in the waters along the runway. One day, I mentioned it to a neighbor who replied, "Yeah, it's great for those who are into fishing, but I never notice that." Well, why not? Is that pleasure reserved only for those who fish and denied to the rest of us? Or do we deny ourselves of these pleasures Life offers us openly and freely?

It is our duty to notice these things. Your duty to yourself — for in doing so, you enlarge yourself and enrich your life. You become an active participant in life and one with all of Life.

As you begin experiencing this oneness and unity of all things — the common bonds we share with all of nature, all people — all feelings of separateness fall away. Fear, loneliness, jealousy, all dissolve in this unity, and we begin to experience the harmony of all things and live abundantly and with gratitude.

How many of you have ever stopped and asked yourself, "What is life?" Not — what is the meaning of life — some abstract concept. But what is life? Are we all separate individuals and species placed on earth to "do our own thing," get as much as we can for ourselves without any concern for other species or people? Are we just here, born, grow up, have families and die? Or is there something more, something other than just earning a living, eeking out an existence?

Many people believe and live as though life is something that just happens to them and as Anthony Robbins tells us, they don't "design" their own life.

That's really funny when you think of how meticulously we design and decorate our homes, the great care we take in choosing our automobiles, the discerning eye we bring to shopping for a wardrobe. Shouldn't we put some of that same energy, attention and care into "designing" the life we want to lead rather than just letting ourselves be tossed about by externals like a ship at sea so that we live basically haphazardly?

When we live haphazardly at the whim of external circumstances, we find ourselves feeling victimized and begin complaining about our circumstances — "Look what happened to me." Well, nothing happened to you. Whatever is in your life, you have created by your choices (even not choosing is a choice), your actions, your attitudes. If you live haphazardly, then you must always wait for something good to happen to you so you can be grateful.

But the best thing of all has already happened to you — You are alive — and gratitude begins with graciously accepting this wondrous gift of Life.

You think you don't have enough money, or you are not beautiful enough? Well, somewhere there is a wealthy person and a beautiful person who did not wake up this morning — and they would give anything in the world to look like you and have your limited financial resources — just to be alive.

So whenever you hear yourself or anyone complaining that "Life is Hard," or "I don't have . . ." or "I wish I could . . ." tell them and yourself — *Life is good.* In fact, wake up every morning and say "Life is good," or "Hello Day . . . What a beautiful day!" Dance around your house or look in the mirror and sing "Good mornin', good mor-or-or-nin', Good mornin', good mornin' to you and you and you and you," that wonderful song from the film *Singin' in the Rain.*

Tell yourself as you greet each day, "This glorious, wonderful, crazy world with all its joy and sadness, ecstasy and pain; all its surprises and opportunities — is serendipitous — and I am here to enjoy it. This day will never come again in the history of the world, so it is my special day to live and enjoy." And you can live it however you choose to. But *choose* to live it; don't just let it happen to you and pass you by, for then, it is gone forever. Embrace today. Bite into it. Caress it. As Thoreau says, *Live deep and suck out all the marrow of life.*

And when you do that, you will find that you automatically begin living with gratitude for everything you have, for this great opportunity called Life, even for the things you don't have that often afflict so many others.

Every time I whined or complained as a child, my father always told me an old Jewish saying — "I complained I had no shoes until I met a man who had no feet." That certainly put things in perspective for me fast.

119

So you can view all of your efforts like Camus' Sisyphus, pushing a huge boulder up a mountainside every day only to have it roll back down every time he approached the summit, or you can live with a grateful appreciation of the natural processes — like a snake growing and cultivating a beautiful skin only to shed it and start all over again, continually growing a new skin again and again and again. You can view your life as an endless, futile labor — or as a process of continual renewal. The choice is yours.

Perhaps one of the reasons so many people fail to take charge of their daily lives simply by changing their attitudes is that many people live as though life were a destination. They are always going to do this when, or think that as soon as I get this or have that, then I'll be able to do what I want. So people are always waiting, biding their time, living a temporary existence — kind of like holding their breath waiting to get to their destination, waiting to get to the "IT" — so they can exhale.

Well — there is no "IT." The HOW is the IT. Life is a process, not a destination, not an end result. *Every moment you are alive is IT.*

Once you realize this, you begin to live in gratitude and that gratitude enriches your life and fosters more gratitude and more richness . . . so that gratitude becomes a way of life.

Then your prayers become prayers of thanksgiving and appreciation rather than of supplication. Prayers uttered out of abundance rather than lack. In fact, what a wonderful way to start and end each day, by saying "Thank you."

But don't just express your gratitude verbally, live it. And the way you live gratitude is by living with wonder and appreciation. Not just appreciation for the richness of your life, but for others too.

For once you begin to celebrate your own life, your own abundance, you can really begin to celebrate others' as well, by caring about and doing things for others, by being glad in their achievements and good fortune, by giving them compliments, an uplifting smile or word. We all need that. It can change a drab, grey day into a bright, sunny one. And all because you decided to be grateful for the beauty and richness you share with all people.

An essential aspect of gratitude that is often so difficult for people is acceptance. For once you have given prayers of thanks, it is important that you learn to accept, to "receive" that good for which you have prayed. So many of us pray for things, and then when we get what we want, we are unable to accept it.

My friend who was suffering from RAS was literally unable to do most simple tasks that required her to use her hands. After months of living with this disability, she attended a conference on Shamanism and decided to have an Inca Shaman from Peru do a healing on her hands. Well, the night before the healing, she called me in the middle of a panic attack and exclaimed, "Oh my God, I'm really going to be healed! What am I going to do?" She was having a very difficult time accepting that. As so many people, she had gotten so used to, so attached to her problem, her limitation, that she actually felt nervous about being without it.

Receiving is difficult for many people. So many of us even find it difficult to accept a compliment. When we do receive one, we bow our heads, or make some excuse or shy away from it, not knowing how to receive the compliment. But receiving is an integral part of gratitude — of opening up to the good we receive and experience in our lives. To accepting the fact that we *are* worth it, we *do* deserve it. That life is supposed to be good, exciting, thrilling — an adventure. And that we are the explorers in this adventure called Life.

There is an old Yiddish saying — "Man plans and God laughs." When my father first told me this, I thought "how cruel." I didn't understand then . . . didn't understand that this process called Life is constantly changing. No matter how much you plan, no matter how tightly you hold onto something, it will change, for that is what life is — change, the unknown . . . that is the adventure.

And if we embark upon this adventure with free will, with our receptors wide open; even though it is unpredictable and full of surprises, we will be grateful for having the ability to make choices and we will exercise it. We will learn to be grateful for all we have. And once we are grateful for what we have, our receptors open wider, allowing even more into our lives until we are so rich and wide open, that ultimately . . . we can open up to our dreams.

When asked how he paints his paintings,
Van Gogh replied —

*I dream my paintings and then
I just paint my dreams.*

Vincent Van Gogh

Part 2

Try not — Do or do not . . .
There is no try.

Yoda / *The Empire Strikes Back*
George Lucas

The future belongs to those who believe
in the beauty of their dreams.

Eleanor Roosevelt

What you can do, or dream you can, begin it,
Boldness has genius, power, and magic in it.

Johann Wolfgang von Goethe

Chapter 12

DARE TO DREAM

The bigger your dreams, the greater your reality. In your dreams, is your power and your strength because your dreams come from the energy source — the core of who you are — your soul.

And don't ever let anyone tell you your dreams are not important or that they are foolish or that they are too big. You can never dream too big — for your dreams are the very substance of God. They are the divinity within you and God is infinite and you are unlimited in possibilities.

You can make your dreams a reality no matter how big, how outrageous, how impossible they may seem. Nothing is impossible. Remember this — the difficult takes time . . . the impossible just takes a little longer.

There are endless stories of people who have succeeded in achieving the impossible. The only difference between these people and you is that they listened to their dreams, respected their dreams, believed in their dreams . . . and acted on them.

So, whatever it is . . . You can do it. You just have to believe you can, want it badly enough, and persist — no matter what. When he was Prime Minister of Great Britain, Winston Churchill addressed a graduating class. He walked up to the podium and began his speech, "Ladies and Gentlemen and all you young graduates. Never, never, never, never, never, never . . . never give up," and returned to his seat to resounding applause, for he had hit upon a basic truth — a core message.

Remember this — Anything . . . no, *Everything* is possible. You just have to view every seeming failure as a learning experience, an opportunity, a guideline pointing you in the right direction, helping you to make the necessary adjustments in your course and find your way. If you persist, you will always succeed.

Philosophers and writers throughout the ages have told us that "If you can dream it, you can achieve it," "If you can conceive of something, then you can do it." Why? Because our dreams take us out of the mundane world into the spirit realm — the fourth dimension where we have superhuman powers — the realm in which we can surpass ourselves as Neitzsche tells us in *Thus Spake Zarathustra* — the realm in which we become the Superman.

Writing almost one hundred years ago, Neitzsche writes that this capacity to surpass ourselves is reserved for the select few. I believe it is in everyone. We all have the capacity to surpass ourselves and achieve great things. And everything great begins with a dream.

Dreams are not just something we experience during sleep and to be analyzed. Dreams are not just for children. Dreams are for everyone. Our dreams are to be realized, not just analyzed or patronized as wishful longings.

There is a real reason why we have dreams. We have dreams so we can achieve them — so we can aspire to something greater than ourselves. We have dreams so we can realize them.

So be proud of your dreams. And don't let anyone tell you they are foolish or meaningless. Embrace your dreams and they will keep you young and vibrant and alive. They will sustain you so that you not only endure, but you prevail. Be moved by your dreams, not intimidated by them.

Everything great begins with a dream. There is greatness in each one of us. So let your spirit soar on the wings of your dreams — and in this, you will be uplifted and will find you can accomplish miracles, just by believing you can.

They can because they think they can.

Virgil

For as he thinketh in his heart, so is he.

King Solomon

Chapter 13

THE Magic of Believing

Belief is exactly that — magic. Deep, firm, un-wavering belief performs miracles. "It sets in motion certain inner forces that enable you to achieve your goals," Claude Bristol tells us in his marvelous book, *The Magic of Believing*.

When he speaks of belief however, he is not referring to an intellectual concept. He is speaking of belief as a way of being — a process. Belief in something larger than yourself of which you are a part. Whether you call this something God, Great Spirit, Universal Energy, Cosmic Mind, The Force or just . . . The Source, is unimportant. What is important is to believe in an orderly universe — a universe that does not deal with us capriciously, but one that functions orderly, according to the laws of nature, of which we are an integral part.

This kind of belief is the basis for all possibilities and functions as a powerful anchor. Out of this, like the trunk of a mighty oak, grow the branches of all our other beliefs — our belief that all things are possible, the belief that we can do anything (or rather, everything), the belief that we *will* succeed.

This kind of belief is rooted in trust and faith. Not religious faith (although it can be), but faith in oneself and the universe of which we are a part. A universe that treats us kindly and with love, and is always on our side. This kind of trust knows no questions, no details, no "what ifs."

This kind of trust knows that the only things that can harm or bother you are those things you are conscious or aware of and that "ignorance is bliss." Not only bliss, but power, for in the "ignoring" of something, we refuse to give it substance, reality or power, and therefore, recenter the power within ourselves. As Claude Bristol reminds us, "We have all heard the story of the man who didn't know it couldn't be done and went ahead and did it."

I'm sure you have all heard of the placebo effect, where two groups of patients are given a pill they are told will make them better. One group however, receives the actual medicine in the pill, the other receives the placebo — and the group receiving the placebo heals just as quickly and as well as the group receiving the actual medicine. Why? Because they believe the pill they are taking will make them better — so it does. As Norman Cousins tells us, "Belief becomes biology." It doesn't matter that the pill contains no medicinal benefits. Their minds tell their bodies it does, so the body responds as if it is being treated medicinally and heals.

Studies done on people with multiple personalities further validate this mind/body connection. When the individual is functioning as one personality, he or she exhibits all the symptoms of diabetes or allergies or asthma. Yet when the individual is functioning as the split or alternate personality, there is no evidence of any of these illnesses. This is irrefutable evidence of the power of the mind.

As the Buddha said centuries ago, "All that we are is the result of what we have thought." Health or disease, success or failure . . . all of these depend more on our beliefs and mental attitudes than on our activities and mental capacities. It's not "what we do, but how we do it," — with what attitude, what belief system we operate from.

Once you realize that, you know that you can do anything you want, as long as you believe you can. Danny Kaye, a gifted actor in the 1940's, was also a very accomplished conductor. Someone once asked him, "How did you know you could do that?" And he replied, "No one ever told me I couldn't."

I remember when I bought my townhouse years ago. I was very young and very näive and knew nothing about the intricacies— the "details" — of buying a home. I only knew that I wanted a home for my son. I found the perfect place and bought it. I signed the papers and gave a deposit on it right away.

As the time approached to close on the house, I discovered that since my income was minimal, I could not qualify for a mortgage. So, I needed to assume the previous owner's mortgage. No problem . . . Until I learned that I had committed to coming up with $30,000 to do this. Gulp! I had only $15,000 if I sold, liquidated and cashed in everything I had. I was still $15,000 short.

Miraculously, a wealthy aunt of mine, who had never before given me money for anything, gave me a gift of $5000 (without knowing I was short of money and needed it), my parents gifted me $5000 (as they told me they had my sister when she bought her house) and my parents loaned me $5000 on a certificate of deposit they had which I subsequently paid the interest on and paid back. Voila! I had my $30,000 and my townhouse — without any figuring or wondering how I would get the money I needed to buy it. I just knew I desperately wanted it, bought it — and saw the deal done, saw me and my son living in it. And so it was.

Claude Bristol writes that, "William James, the father of modern psychology in America, declared that often our faith (belief) in advance of a doubtful undertaking is the only thing that can assure its successful conclusion. Man's faith, according to James, acts on the powers above him as a claim and creates its own verification. In other words, the thought becomes literally father to the fact."

This concept was not new then and is not new now to the burgeoning New Age movement. Outstanding thinkers throughout the centuries have told us that man, through his mind, can shape events and control matter.

We can do this most efficiently by activating our conscious minds as well as our subconscious mind. So in addition to our belief system, it is often helpful if we engage in certain rituals or ceremonies. These can be formalized rituals, as in a church or temple or other kind of society (Native American or Shamanic tradition, for example). Or they can be your own personalized rituals and symbolic gestures that you create for yourself. These rituals or gestures can be as simple as doing something three times, or kissing a picture, or praying every morning, or even just facing east when you pray to something; or as complex as an entire ceremony or ritual you make up for yourself with things that have special significance for you.

When I first began writing this book, for example, I felt it was essential (good luck, if you will) for it to be eighteen chapters, (because in ancient Hebrew there were no numbers, so each letter had a numerical equivalent and the Hebrew word for Life, *Chai*, was numerically equivalent to eighteen), but I didn't want to artificially impose such a limitation on it. My feeling about this was so strong however, that I was certain the book would fall into a pattern of eighteen chapters . . . It had to. Happily, when I completed the book, it did come to eighteen chapters. These personal rituals can be very powerful and effective in helping you get what you want by setting unseen forces in motion.

How? Claude Bristol explains it this way: "These rituals and ceremonies are all designed to appeal to the emotions and to create a mystical picture in the minds of the beholders. These rituals, no matter what the setting, are there to hold your attention and to link the hidden meanings of these symbols with the particular ideas that are to be implanted in your mind."

So, belief — the magic of believing — acts not only as a solid anchor for us in whatever we decide to do or "go for" by rooting and grounding us in a surety, a certainty, an unshakable confidence that we will succeed; but belief is also a powerful motivator. Like a generator, your firmly held belief is the power source, the energy source, that sets your dreams in motion and stimulates the process of realization that was begun by your imagination and activated by your dreams.

Belief, coupled with passion is the purest fuel there is. It is totally undiluted and untainted — pure 100% octane — and this is what guarantees your success in a process which begins with a dream and culminates in the reality of that dream.

CHANCES
aren't given. They're taken.

Source Unknown

Be bold, and mighty forces will
come to your aid.

Basil King

Chapter 14

PURSUE YOUR PASSION AND NEW POSSIBILITIES WILL AWAKEN

Get excited about your dreams. That excitement is what propels them forward to the next step in actualizing them. Your passion is what transforms your thoughts into action.

Passion makes you bold and willing to take risks for what you believe in. Passion obliterates any fear of failure and sees only success — only the dreams realized. For if you realize that there is no such thing as failure, only experience to learn from, then you will understand that the only failure is not to try at all, not to dare.

Anthony Robbins tells us that those who have succeeded the most have also failed the most. As I mentioned, the year Babe Ruth broke the world's record for the most home runs, he also broke the record for the most strike-outs. The important thing is getting up to bat.

There are thousands of stories of people just like you and me who have done "the impossible" — have achieved their dreams. Some of them even lost it all, often more than once, and came back even stronger to achieve even greater dreams and greater success.

Sure there are also stories of those who didn't succeed, who got knocked down by obstacles and stayed down. But the choice is yours — which do you want to use as your role models? As Robert Schuller, a long-time proponent of possibility thinking tells us "Tough times never last, but tough people do." People who have faith, who have a dream and passion, not only last . . . they prevail.

So be willing to take risks for what you are passionate about, believe in and dream of. Open up to your passion, let yourself be carried along by the surge of energy it creates. Be willing to lose yourself in it — for in doing that — you will find yourself.

I have a friend who, thirteen years ago, took a trip to Paris where she discovered a creative side of herself she never knew existed. She had a burning passion for writing. Upon returning to the States, she quit her $70,000 a year job, struggled for many years with this new identity and near poverty, with rejection and criticism from nearly everyone who knew her and thought she was mad until she finally had a nervous breakdown. And now, thirteen years later, she has come out the other end of the tunnel into the light. She is happy, successful and whole for the first time in her entire life. She is doing what she truly wants to do, what she was meant to do — poetry therapy and journaling at nursing homes, with AIDS patients and lesbian groups, while those who criticized her and made fun of her are no further along on their journey of self-realization and fulfillment. By totally abandoning herself to her passion, by trusting it and losing herself in it, she ultimately found her true self — her whole self. . . her reality.

For when you are passionate about something, you don't approach it with your mind, but with your heart and soul. And since your soul is the source of everything that you are, it will never betray you or let you down. It will always lead you to what is right and good for you.

Just trust the process. For it is a process just as surely as is the caterpillar going into the cocoon and emerging a butterfly; just as the snake shedding its skin to begin life over and fresh; just as the mighty oak grows from the little acorn despite having weathered many, often brutal winter storms.

So listen to your "umbelini." It will always tell you what to do and guide you. Claude Bristol tells us in *The Magic of Believing*, "when you have that knowing inside of you, fear has vanished and the obstruction to a continued life of all good removed."

When I say "lose yourself in your passion," I am not talking about frivolous or reckless passion, but a deep, burning desire. Ted Turner, the Vice President of Time Warner, President of CNN, TNT, World Cup recipient, former husband of Jane Fonda, and the list goes on and on . . . started out as the son of a sign painter. As he kept venturing into new territory, trying new things because he had a dream — several dreams, as a matter of fact — each one bigger than the one before, he didn't listen to his detractors, his critics who said he was crazy, that he could lose everything. He saw his dreams as real. So he did whatever he had to, to make the outer reality match the inner reality he already saw.

145

It doesn't mean it was easy or that he succeeded the first time, or the second or even the tenth, but he never gave up. Like a good navigator, he kept adjusting his course with each new setback. And there were many. He followed his vision — always. Yes — that's it. He dared to be a visionary. He dared to "see" and believe in what he saw.

Just like Ted Turner, you too can have anything you want in life, "provided" as Claude Bristol tells us, "you are willing to make that objective the burning desire of your life."

Perhaps the title of this chapter should be "Dare to Live" or "Dare to Be Truly Alive," for that is where the real fear lies. So many people are afraid of the "f" word — failure — (which we have already established does not exist), so afraid of dying, that they never really live at all.

As Elizabeth Kubler-Ross tells us, the people who scream the loudest on their deathbeds are those who haven't really lived at all. They have been observers of life, not active participants. Nobody wants to die, but we are all going to. So at least, while you are alive, allow yourself to experience the rapture of being alive. So when you do finally pass on, you will know that you have truly lived.

So smell your dreams, see them, touch them, taste them — let them become real for you. So real that there is no "if" only "when;" no "how" only "doing." For passion is energy and energy creates momentum and this momentum generates a surge of power and resources you never even knew you possessed.

Like persistence and discipline, those elusive qualities that most of us think we lack, that erupt spontaneously out of our passion like jungle growth in the rain forest. Not just one or two, but an explosion — so all details are swept aside and we see only the final outcome — success.

I'm sure you've all heard the saying "Success is 10% inspiration and 90% perspiration." Persistence is the engine that keeps the entire process going until its successful completion. The energy for that persistence is born out of passion . . . and nothing can stand in its way.

Like a dam that has broken so the water gushes forth, there is no stopping it. If there are obstacles, the water will go around it, over it, under it — or just plain wear it down — but it will get to where it is going. There is never any doubt about that.

And as you pursue your passion, you will find new opportunities serendipitously arising. Suddenly just the "right" people will appear in your life to help you — or you will be in just the right place at the right time. Small miracles, large miracles will begin happening to help you achieve your dream. For once you take action motivated by passion, you set in motion a whole series of events that magnetize everything you need to you.

And passion sets all dreams in motion — not just major ones. There are minor dreams also, occasional dreams. They are all important. The same passion goes into each one as living with passion becomes a way of life and the same magnetism occurs even with the smallest dream or wish or thought —just like a magnet equally attracts a tiny hairpin or a huge iron bar. The process is the same . . . the result guaranteed.

A popular motivational slogan on the benefits of risk-taking tells us, "You cannot discover new oceans unless you are willing to lose sight of the shore." This willingness to take risks is born out of passion and the thing you should be most passionate about is living. It's worth it.

*Treat someone as if they are
what they could become,
and that is what
one day they shall be.*

Johann Wolfgang von Goethe

We should expect the best,
and so live that the best may become
a part of our experience.

The Science of Mind
Ernest Holmes

Chapter 15

Expect The Best and Get it

Why would anyone do anything unless they expect the best? Unless they expect to get what they want, to achieve their desired goal? To do anything other than expect that, is to waste your time, energy and money. Yet, that is precisely what many of us do.

We do things without ever really expecting to succeed. Oh, we *hope* to succeed, yes (but hope is so tentative) — but we do not *expect* to succeed. Why should you even bother doing it then? If you don't truly expect yourself to succeed, why should anyone else? Why should God?

I remember one day, I went to the Publix supermarket in Miami and asked the cashier to check my lotto ticket. I felt certain I had won. When she told me I hadn't, I was genuinely surprised and visibly shocked and asked, "Are you sure?" She, of course, thought I was crazy. I didn't even have one of the winning numbers. It wasn't even a near miss. But I expect to win every week I buy a ticket (although that week, the feeling was particularly strong). Otherwise, I wouldn't buy one.

But many people are afraid to expect the best. Afraid they will be disappointed if they don't succeed. So what if you get disappointed. Just move on to the next and the next and the next opportunity . . . expecting the best each time. Then you are always living each day with this wonderful feeling of anticipation. What a way to live!

A friend of mine had written a science fiction book for teenagers and decided to begin sending it out to publishers, ones she had carefully selected and often, had spoken to personally. I got really excited for her. "I have a feeling one of these is going to be the one," I told her when she sent it out to the first two. My enthusiasm became contagious and she was soon swept up in it. Giddy with anticipation, she was smiling more, laughing more, happier than she had been in years, enjoying not only the process of trying to find a publisher for her book, but enjoying every day. Her entire attitude lightened up as she did her daily chores and job.

When she received a rejection from the first one about a month or two later, I said, "Maybe the other one will be IT. I think so." So she again rode the wave of my enthusiasm. Well, when she received a rejection from the second, she called me very annoyed and declared, "I'm not going to listen to you anymore. I'm not going to let myself get excited ever again." I couldn't believe my ears.

"You mean to tell me you are willing to give up that wonderful feeling of anticipation and excitement you've been feeling, the happiness and joy you've been living with these last few months just so you won't be disappointed?"

"Yes," she replied defiantly and hung up — as though she were hurting me and it was my loss.

Think of it. How often we live with low expectations and deny ourselves the pleasure and excitement of the anticipation of joy and success just so we won't be disappointed. Why not just open the door and invite disappointment in? For that is what we are doing — welcoming, expecting, paving the way for disappointment.

In fact, all of the great philosophers, sages and the self-help writers of today tell us that our expectations affect everything in our life — for nothing is insignificant. That's why it is so important what we think and believe and expect.

A few days ago, I was running in the morning and thinking about the chapter on abundance. As I was thinking about joy and wonder, I looked down and saw something big and round and yellow on the ground and exclaimed to myself, "Isn't that nice — A Happy Face!" Well of course, it wasn't a happy face at all. It was a perfectly round dry leaf; but I saw what I expected to see, what my attention was focused on.

Later that week, I was feeling particularly lonely, missing two of my closest friends who live in France and Sweden. When I returned home from my run and picked up the phone to listen to the messages I had received on my "memory call" service, I heard the recording say, "Welcome to lonely call service." Well, of course it didn't say that. It said "Welcome to memory call service," which I have heard thousands of times since I've gotten the service, but that morning, I heard what I expected to hear, what my energy was focused on.

In the small and grand things of life, we see what we expect to see, hear what we expect to hear, get what we expect to get, and become what we expect to be. So — always expect the best.

Michelle Weiner-Davis, in her book *Fire Your Shrink,* says that the single most important thing that most determines how a student will do in college is not his previous grades, not his standardized test scores, but his expectation of how well he will do.

If you expect nothing, you often get nothing; or see whatever you do receive as nothing. My cousin enjoys going to Las Vegas occasionally to gamble. Last year, she won $1000. When I found out she had won, I was really happy for her and called and said, "I hear you won $1000. Congratulations! You are so lucky." To which she replied, "Oh yeah, if I'm so lucky, how come I didn't win the jackpot?"

Expecting nothing is disappointing. Expecting the worst is depressing. If you expect the worst, you often get it. My ex-boyfriend always wanted to be prepared for the worst — that way he felt he could never be disappointed. So he spent a large part of his time and energy preparing for and focusing on the worst. The end result, of course, was that much of his life was a disappointment because he was always living with a constant awareness of and catering to "the worst." So he never got to feel, experience, enjoy the best. He missed out on the "rapture of being alive." For in trying to eliminate the possibility of disappointment, you also eliminate the possibility of real joy.

So get excited. Don't be afraid to effervesce and gush. Open yourself up wide and enjoy the anticipation and learn to react to disappointment (when it does come) with surprise rather with than depression and devastation. When you react to disappointment in this way, with surprise (which becomes an automatic response when you expect the best), you will always move on to the next expectation and keep your sense of wonder.

Instead of thinking about all the things that can go wrong, think of all the things than can go right. Worrying cancels joy. It takes all the pleasure out of anticipation. So, once you do something, proceed with faith and belief in the best . . . and enjoy the process. For that's all life is — a process.

When you expect the best, you open yourself up to doing your best and can bring out the best in others as well. You become part of the energy flow — the give and take of the universe. Without this expectation, this energy flow is blocked and cannot flow smoothly, freely, fluidly. Your low or negative expectation stops the flow in and out, to and from you and others and the universe and God.

Often, people are afraid to expect the best and get excited because they are afraid they will look foolish if they don't get what they want or anticipate.

A friend of mine recently was matched up with a prominent judge through a dating service. They exchanged long-distance calls for several weeks and grew to know each other and like each other. They practically lived for those calls. Their conversations were romantic, passionate, intimate, full of laughter, discovery . . . calls that created a kind of breathless anticipation of their meeting. These conversations of exquisite beauty involved them totally in a kind of passionate courtship for weeks and they decided they wanted to get married. Everyone thought they were crazy. I didn't. Anything's possible. They were delirious with delight, literally living in sheer ecstasy for those four or five weeks.

Even though the fireworks fizzled when they met, they both — for four or five exquisite weeks — experienced the "rapture of being alive." Isn't that better than never knowing "rapture?"

William Faulkner writes in *Wild Palms*, "If I had to chose between pain and nothing, I would always choose pain." You've all heard the saying, "Better to have loved and lost, than never to have loved at all." Isn't it better to experience the incomparable ecstasy of anticipation, of expecting the best, than never to allow yourself to feel anything just so you won't be disappointed?

Yes, there were those people who thought my friend looked foolish. But not I and not she. There were those who told her she was foolish to let herself get so excited. Personally, I think they are the foolish ones, not my friend.

For there are always two possibilities to everything. Either you will get what you want or you won't. So why not expect the former?

When I was living in Israel, a friend of mine told me that the University of Tel Aviv was looking for English instructors — people with a minimum of two years' teaching experience and a Masters Degree. At the time, I had neither, but I thought, "Why not?" and went and applied anyway. I figured the worst that could happen is I wouldn't get the job. Well, I not only got the job, but I was the only one he hired . . . and I became his best instructor, the one whose class he had all his other instructors come observe. Although everyone thought I must have slept with him to get the position, I knew I got it because I expected to get it — despite the fact that I had none of the requisite qualifications. And this was not an isolated incident. This has happened to me over and over and over in my life.

For when you expect the best, when you make that expectation a way of life; you see and experience only good things and the best, since your expectation brings out the best in you and in other people, no matter what the situation.

Years ago, I was hitching around Europe with another girl. Late at night, two Italian truck drivers stopped (in two separate trucks) and offered to give us each a ride to our destination, where we would rendezvous the next morning. So we went.

The next thing I knew, I was alone on a dark, deserted mountain road in the middle of the night with an Italian truck driver who spoke no English. Although you may not be surprised, I certainly was when he pulled off the road and began to fondle me. We were isolated. No one would have heard me scream. With nothing to stop him from proceeding with his intention to rape me, he stopped. Why?

I believe it was because of my innocence born of my expectation of him and everyone to be their best. Not just a passive innocence — a state of being — but rather, an active innocence; an active trust, not born of not knowing, but of choosing to know and see only the good. And this active quality of it is what elicits the good. My totally unwavering reaction, more of surprise than anything else is what elicits the best in people. For I believe it brings them back to themselves, to their soul, the very core of their being . . . where they are always at their best.

Now you may be saying, "It could have gone the other way also." Yes, it could have. But that was not my experience. It was not my lesson. My lesson was in the experience I had, so I could share it with others in this book, to help others see the enormous power of authenticity and of expecting the best.

And this was not an isolated incident. I found myself in similar compromising situations many times. In Germany where two young guys took me and the girl hitching with me home with them and gave us their apartment for the night and they slept at a friend's; and in France where a much older, very suave, good looking French doctor shared his hotel bed with me and agreed to do nothing more than hold me all night. A Frenchman! This goes totally against all stereotypes.

Now, I am not advocating that anyone get themselves into these situations. But if you ever are in them, I can't think of a better place to come from than a place of trust and belief in the best in each of us.

Difficult, you say? If you approach it with your mind, yes. But if you arrive there through your heart — no. Anne Frank, despite the horrors she experienced at the hands of the Nazis, wrote in her diary, *In spite of everything, I still believe that people are really good at heart.* She understood.

For I truly believe the Goethe quote at the beginning of this chapter. If you treat people as if they are what they are capable of becoming, you help them become what they are capable of being. People's and life's response to you become a self-fulfilling prophecy. So accept life's best and then get out of your own way and let it happen.

Especially with your dreams. For once your passion has propelled you to take action on your dreams, your expectation of the best will assure you of getting what you want. And the greatest dream of course, is for love — for a life that is full and rich and rewarding. Expect it . . . and surely, you will live it.

An integral being knows without going,
sees without looking, and accomplishes
without doing.

Lao Tzu

*It is not a matter of **if** you will succeed,*
Only when.

Thea Patton Rosmini

Chapter 16

LiVE AS if

Once you expect the best, it is easy to live as if. What do I mean by "live as if?" I mean that whatever you want in life; live as if you already have it, did it, accomplished it, are it.

Goethe's quote admonishing us to treat people as if they already are what they can be and in so doing, help them become what they are capable of being, applies to our attitude towards ourselves as well as others. If we act, in our lives, as if we already have what we desire, as if we already are what we ought to or could be, then we become that which we wish to be — the "if" slips away and it becomes only a matter of "when" the external reality will catch up with the inner one we have already accepted and are living.

Just think of all the time, energy and resources we free up when we live as if and let go of fear, worry, anxiety and doubt. Do you have any idea how much energy it takes to worry about things? To be afraid? To always doubt and question the possible outcomes? Imagine constantly pulling a wagon with uneven, thick, primitive solid wooden wheels behind you. And as you pull it, something new gets heaped on the pile at each station you pass. Then imagine how good you feel once you leave the wagon and all its cargo in the station and just ship it to your final destination, with no more thought of it, certain it will arrive just as you packed it.

That is the experience of living as if. A feeling of complete freedom, for you are traveling with no baggage. How many of us have gone on trips and taken too much luggage that we had to drag and shlep on and off the plane, the train, etc.? And then, we finally go on a trip and decide to pack just one small suitcase on rollers. What a pleasure. I don't know about you, but I breathe a sigh of relief and wonder why I didn't do it sooner.

So stop worrying and begin to live as if. You will travel much farther, easier, more comfortably, and certainly much happier through life if you do.

Many of us are actually afraid to live as if — to feel too good or happy. We feel almost as if we are being arrogant and in this, tempting the hand of fate, tempting God. We believe we are supposed to struggle and worry, and if we are not, we feel almost like a kid who is getting away with something. So we create problems. We have a good job and worry about losing it. Our health is fine and we worry about getting sick or dying.

We make ourselves meek and small and unobtrusive, hoping God won't notice how happy we are, how well things are going, for us . . . hoping he will leave us be and not give us any problems, not test us to see how strong, happy and good we really are. So we are afraid to be too happy, too exuberant — to shine too bright — thinking perhaps, we will dim others with our light and make God angry and want to really test us — to "show us."

To show us what? Think of it. Show us not to be happy? Why? God loves us. And you can never dim anyone with your light. The brighter your light, the more you illuminate others and the world. God wants us to be happy, healthy and strong so we can help others and make the world more beautiful and livable.

Unfortunately, most people have internalized the concept of an authoritarian, anthropomorphic God who sits in constant judgement of us. But God is not vindictive or judgemental like in the *Old Testament*. Apparently, the stories of Job and the sacrifice of Abraham are so deeply embedded in our collective psyches, that we feel we must be constantly and severely tested to see if we are worthy.

Worthy of what? Love? Happiness? Health? Success? Of course we are worthy. Just by dint of being born — of being here as part of God's creation. Our worthiness lies in our beingness.

If you look to Eastern religion and philosophy, you will understand that the Buddha resides in every one of us. Even Christianity tells us that "the kingdom of God is within." There is no authority figure hovering over us and judging us, always holding us accountable. We are part of the universal energy — the All-Good — the Force, the Spirit, the Energy that is within and suffuses everything. Even modern physics confirms this — the universality of an energy that interconnects all of us — everything on this planet.

So when you live your life as if, your actions are like dominoes affecting everything and everyone else and affecting your own Self — everything about you. For all your actions are interconnected . . . beginning with a dream and culminating in the realization of that dream; the ultimate and all inclusive dream of course being, a happy, fulfilling, healthy life — a life filled with love.

*. . . love is the most important thing
in the world. It may be important to great
thinkers to examine the world, to explain
and despise it. But I think it is only
important to love the world, not to despise
it, not for us to hate each other, but to
be able to regard the world and ourselves
and all beings with love, admiration and
respect.*

Siddhartha
Hermann Hesse

Love cures people — both the ones who give it and the ones who receive it.

Dr. Karl Menninger

Chapter 17

LOVE IS THE ANSWER

No matter what the question or problem . . . Love is the answer. It begins with your Self and then radiates outward. But without self-love — if you live with fear, separation and anger — the light that shines through you becomes obstructed. As you allow these negative emotions to dwell and fester within you, your pores become clogged, so little or no light can enter into or emanate out from you.

But if you decide to live with love, "to think and live as though everyone could read the one and see the other," as Og Mandino suggests we do, then each one of us, individually and collectively, could eliminate all wars, all conflicts, all anger and hatred — almost all problems. Even physical, for it is now finally becoming an accepted truth that almost all physiological ailments (even aging!) have their roots in our psyche. Crime would be eliminated, prisons would become unnecessary and lawyers would become a thing of the past (oh dear — how dreadful!).

So do as Marlo Morgan in her book *Mutant Message Down Under* tells us the aborigines do in Australia. By communicating telepathically, they train their young from a very early age to think only nice thoughts, to have only feelings of love. Every time a child is playing with another and has a selfish thought, he looks up and sees all the adults glaring at him, since they can read his mind. Needless to say, all negative thoughts are eliminated very quickly.

Well, you can read all your own thoughts. So be your own elder and eradicate all negative thinking from your mind and replace it with thoughts of love and kindness. I tried it, acting and thinking as though everyone could read my mind. And it really works.

And once you become Love, that is all you will be able to transfer and convey to your children and those around you, because out of a thing, comes whatever is inside it. When you begin to live with . . . no . . . be permeated by and suffused with love, all the things we have been talking about in this book will fall into place as it becomes a natural reaction, an automatic response for you to let go, like yourself, live as if, expect the best, to forgive . . . for Love becomes what you are.

Love does not see faults and blemishes. Loves sees only the good — like looking through a filtered lens.

I remember when I was living in Israel and my cousin fixed me up with a scientist from the Weitzman Institute. He was slightly pudgy; had pale, freckled skin; thinning, curly, red hair and wore glasses. Without a doubt, he was the least attractive guy I had ever been out with and I was upset with my cousin for fixing me up with him.

However, he was her fiancé's best friend, so somehow I wound up going out with him again on a double date with them. Later that evening, he and I went back to his apartment and we began talking and he played piano for me long into the night. Lost in his music, I began to see and relate to the sensitive, beautiful musician that he was in his soul. I proceeded to fall passionately in love with him, finding him so sexy and alluring that I literally could not keep my hands off him. If this hadn't happened to me personally, I would never have believed such a total transformation possible.

As I witness, over and over again, the transformative power of love, I am always newly amazed at how powerful and complete it is. A friend of mine, whose mother is paranoid/schizophrenic and has been in and out of institutions practically her whole life, hated her mother. When I met her eight years ago, my friend was consumed by blatant anger, hostility and resentment towards her mother.

Then my friend met a man, fell in love and got married. Over the next five years, I observed the most amazing process take place — I watched as the love she experienced in her life filled her up so much that it literally pushed out all the hatred, anger and resentment, in effect, extinguishing these negative emotions. There was just no more room for them in her life anymore. The light inside her illuminated the darkness and in doing so, obliterated it. And the interesting thing is that this was not a conscious decision on her part. It just happened naturally, effortlessly, as a consequence of being filled up with love.

For love really does conquer all, as the Latin philosopher Virgil tells us. Love knows no blame (and this includes ourselves, for we are always so much harder on ourselves, more critical of ourselves than of anyone else). The natural response of love to a wrong or an error is one of understanding and forgiveness. Understanding that no one says to himself, "I'm going to be mean when I grow up," or "I'm going to hurt my children, ignore my parents, beat my spouse, or have a terrible marriage." All these negative experiences are merely a result of that person's own weakness or pain, not an evil nature. For I believe that there is no evil as Rilke tells us — that there are only princes, (ugly frogs or dragons under a spell) "waiting to see us once beautiful and brave; that everything terrible in our life is in its deepest being, something helpless that wants help from us."

So love forgives. Jesus admonished us to "Love our enemies." People often ask me, "How do you do that? It's so difficult to love your enemies." But if you are coming from love; not a romantic, individualized love, but what the Greeks called AGAPE — a love that comes from the spirit, a love and appreciation of all life and the interconnectedness of all things — then it becomes impossible not to forgive. Forgiveness becomes the only reaction possible, because you understand that these people, your "enemies," are acting out of their own weakness and pain. And with this understanding, how can you have any other response?

How do you open up to become love you ask? Sometimes it can be spontaneously triggered by an epiphany — that "moment in the rose garden." But most of the time, it is a process — an opening, like the petals of a flower. Whether this process is precipitated by a trauma or merely a deep desire to grow, it always begins with self-love and like, and blossoms into a joyous, wondrous journey that culminates in the realization of your dreams.

Love is the binding element that allows all the steps in this process to come together. How does love accomplish this? Perhaps because love is the ultimate letting go — for in love, you surrender to the process, the God within you, the laws of nature of which you are a part.

But letting go is only half the process. For when you let go, you release whatever is holding you back, any negative forces in your life. You empty yourself.

But then, you must fill yourself up again — with love — AGAPE. And when you are replete with love, you enter the flow of the abundance of the universe out of your own fullness.

Then you can surrender to and accept the miracles that are out there waiting to happen in your life. Miracles that are happening all the time, even now, but need the light of love and the acceptance of child-mind . . . serendipity to experience them.

As I was running this morning thinking about what I was going to write in this chapter, about accepting the miracles in our lives, a miracle happened to me. Suddenly, I knew — not wished, not was "going to" be, not planning to be — but I knew, for the first time in my life that *I am a writer*. No longer that "I am writing a book or a story," or that "I am writing now" or "writing again" (which is what all aspiring writers are always saying to themselves and others), but that I *am* a writer. I felt it surely, certainly and wholly in my gut.

And as I was experiencing this feeling, I passed a Royal Poinciana tree, hung low and broad like a Bonsai. It was in full bloom with rich orange flowers. I have passed this tree hundreds of times in the last three years. But today, for the first time, just as I was swelling up, becoming replete with the overwhelming feeling of love, of knowing without a doubt that I am a writer, that I am doing what I have always wanted to do, what I've always known I was meant to do — the sweetest fragrance wafted up through my nose to my brain, flooding me with the sensation. And I sighed, "Ah — the sweet smell of success. . . so this is what it feels like to accomplish your goal, to realize your dream, to feel complete."

It is said that the sense of smell is the most powerful, most enduring of our five senses because it is a pure and immediate sensation that goes directly to the brain. That's why aromatherapy is becoming such a popular form of therapy now, as it was in ancient times. The ancients knew that those things we experience through our other senses last hours, days, weeks or years, perhaps — but the associations made through those things we smell often last a lifetime.

How fortunate I am to have, at that moment, experienced the synchronicity of my epiphany and that fragrance. To have deposited in my psyche, that neuro-association of exquisite sweetness with accomplishment, with achieving my dream — an association that will remain with me for a lifetime. How magical — how serendipitous.

And the end of all our exploring
Will be to arrive where we started
And know the place for the first time.

"Little Gidding"
Four Quartets
T.S. Eliot

The child is the father of man.

William Wordsworth

Chapter 18

CHILD MIND
· · · SERENDIPITY

Serendipity is energy. It is a life force — an inter-active *chi* — a way of experiencing . . . of moving through life.

Like child-mind, it is organic. For when you look at a child, really watch him, what do you see? You see an aliveness — a "NOW"ness — a beingness that shouts *I am* every single moment.

Child-mind is a "me"ness that is, at the same time, an "everything"ness because the toddler merges with everything, giving its total undivided attention to all . . . one thing at a time.

For so many years, I was not "into" toddlers. In fact, while I was so caught up in the pressures of making a living, bringing up my son, running a business and being in a very stressful relationship, I found toddlers rather annoying; their movements erratic, the sounds they make mere noise and gobble-di-gook.

But recently, my niece had a baby and we got to spend Thanksgiving together and I found myself totally captivated by her nine-month-old son who was big and rather precocious. Watching him walk, no waddle, around the living room gasping in delight, "Huh! Huh!" at everything he saw, touched and heard was pure joy as I experienced the wonder of seeing his total involvement in and oneness with all things.

And I watched and I learned and I was brought back to myself. Back to child-mind, which is focused, intense, immediate. Child-mind, that is beautiful and wise in its purity and clarity. Child-mind that is unmuddled, direct and can teach us so much.

Teach us simplicity. For in simplicity, is great wisdom and strength as all the Eastern religions and great sages have told us. The most difficult thing to do is write simply, think simply, live simply — for to do this, we must penetrate to the core of things, to the basics. That is where the meaning, the profundity lies . . . at the very core of a thing distilled down to its bare essence.

But in our complex society, the core has been crusted over with so many layers of impasto splattered on like thick oil paint, so that the core, the simple basics are often lost or forgotten.

We can learn from toddlers how important it is never to lose that sense of wonder and excitement at living for that is what keeps us young and healthy and beautiful and alive. For when you live with this sense of the magic and wonder of being alive, you are always living with this feeling of anticipation that at any moment something wonderful is about to happen.

My mother and her friends are often amused by me —
sometimes even annoyed. "You are always so excited about
something or other," they tell me, especially when I
seemingly have nothing at all to be excited about. Of course
I am excited. I'm excited about living — being alive — about
the next something wonderful that I know is about to happen
and it always does because I expect it to.

Like a horse who has taken off its blinder, I am able to
see and appreciate all the wonderful little miracles all around
me — the magic and wonder and mystery of being alive. I am
able to say "Yes" to it and enjoy it. Enjoy the whole process
that is life. For every day — every act — every thought is a
brushstroke on the canvas of your life. You are a work of art
that you are constantly creating anew every day. So
everything matters.

It is important to get excited, to wonder, to maintain a
sense of the mystery of things. For this fosters a sense of our
own mystery. Ernest Holmes tells us that healthy illusions are
essential to our well-being. They enable us to dream of things
and accomplish things we never could otherwise. Our healthy
illusions give us energy and propel us forward, upward and
outward, which all ultimately lead inward — to the very
center of our being . . . to the resources and God within us.

Child-mind can open us up to passion and intensity. It
can show us how to be totally involved in and responsive to
life with a "nowness" that most adults have forgotten.

I'm sure you've all heard the Latin phrase, *carpe
diem,* admonishing us to "seize the day," to revel in the
moment. This phrase is not only a call to take action in our
lives, but to experience the moment, to live in and enjoy
"now." For Now, this moment, is all we have, all that is real,
all that we can change, affect or influence. The past is

finished, the future hasn't happened yet. Now is all we have. That's why, as Deepak Chopra tells us, it is called "the present."

Children live totally in "now," giving everything to whatever they are doing at the moment. That's why they "sleep like a baby" and most of the rest of us don't. Because children are constantly replenished, always renewing themselves with their immediacy — their "present-ness," while most of us deplete ourselves remorsing over the past or worrying about the future, neither of which we can do anything about. The present moment is the only thing we can create and shape — not by worrying, but by living it fully, and in that way, we create the future we want. For what you do, think, believe now are the building blocks, the very foundation of your future.

So concentrate on right now and you too will be able to "sleep like a baby." For sleep is when the body — the total person — repairs and renews itself. Neitzsche tells us in *Thus Spake Zarathustra* that "Sleep is one of the highest virtues" of the Superman, of man developed to his highest potential — for only one who lives each day well and fully, only one who has found inner peace and balance, can "sleep like a baby" at night.

Which brings me to an often overlooked attribute of child-mind — balance. Living in "now" is often only thought of in terms of a visible, kinetic energy. But children are also so balanced, so centered that they embody the two seemingly opposing aspects of living in the "now" — the excited frenzy of activity, wonder and discovery; as well as that stillness, that intense focus, that quiet and total involvement in whatever they are doing in the moment.

This dynamic of movement and stillness, this total absorption in the activity you are engaged in is very Zen-like.

Perhaps children are the true original Zen masters, for they embody all the qualities the Zen masters do in a way that may seem much more accessible to many than that of the Zen masters.

They embody receptiveness and flexibility, what in Zen is often known as non-attachment. Child-mind is open to anything, for everything is wondrous to children. They are willing to change directions and focus, to let go of something they are involved in for something more wondrous and something else even more compelling.

Now I am not suggesting that we frivolously flit from one endeavor to another. But a willingness to let go of something when it no longer serves our best interests — a flexibility that enables us to be non-attached to the outcome of something we have been working on, even something we have put all our time, passion and energy into — to explore the possibility of a greater good; that is liberating. It frees us to explore, to try, to experiment, to be willing, even happy, to embrace the unexpected as perhaps, an even better opportunity.

Anthony Robbins tells us that many of the greatest discoveries were made as a result of dismal failures, of a willingness to change directions and let go of an expected outcome. Those people who were willing to be flexible, to alter their course or outcome, often serendipitously arrived at a new outcome, equally (if not more) satisfying than they one they intended.

According to Tony Robbins, the man who discovered the 3-M post-it notes was actually searching for an adhesive that would last forever. Instead, he came up with the post-its — the little pieces of adhesive paper that can be easily pulled up without leaving a mark and placed somewhere else . . . serendipity.

Child-mind is patient and persistent. How many times does a toddler stand up and fall down, only to get up again and again and again until it learns how to walk? This persistence of toddlers is characterized by a total commitment to what they are doing, a patience that is willing to be wholly absorbed in accomplishing what they want to. They are not thinking of what they will do next or when they will finish. They are 100% involved in what they are doing — and because of their intensity and focus — they are patient.

On Sunday, I went to the beach with a friend of mine who grew up in Switzerland and spent long hours hiking in the Swiss Alps. We walked three or four miles along the beach to the lighthouse at the very tip of Biscayne Bay — and then back. Had I been alone, I would have lasted maybe one mile, a half hour at the most; certainly not four hours in the searing afternoon sun.

I marveled at my friend's stamina, her endurance, her incredible patience. Since I have a very fast metabolism and tend to be hyper, I was truly in awe of my friend's patience — how slowly and deliberately she moved; how much she enjoyed every moment of our time spent walking on the beach together.

It is by watching my friend, who is very innocent, simple and child-like, that I discovered something very significant about child-mind . . . that child-mind and living in "now" means not only activity and frenzy, but is also quiet and still — and in that is its tremendous energy and intensity and passion; the intensity and passion and power of focus and total involvement. (Isn't that the principle behind the telescope and the laser — the power of the intensity of focus?) During our entire day together, my friend had no thought of anything else, of what she was going to do after, no rush to finish; she had no thought of finishing because she was too busy being in process, too absorbed in her total, non-distracted abandon to her present activity. And that was nice.

This discovery brought me back to serendipity . . . to the serenity that I often forget about that is found in serendipity. The serenity of the balance of movement and stillness — the serenity of that still point from which everything emanates and where all things meet — like the hub of a wheel or the fulcrum of a seesaw.

Yesterday, when I woke up, I did not know what I was going to write in this chapter. I felt something important that I didn't yet know needed to be said. When I went running, I discovered it — the yin and the yang of child-mind — the motion and the stillness, the flexibility and steadfastness, the balance of opposites contained within the whole . . . serendipity.

I was originally going to write about balance in a separate chapter. A chapter in which I discuss homeostasis — the natural response of our bodies to heal themselves — to return to a state of balance and health if we just allow our bodies to function according to the laws of nature and don't interfere.

I was going to elaborate on balance as something internal, not something we get from outside of us. A friend of mine was suffering from panic attacks. She kept going to doctors, seminars, conferences, saying, "I wish I knew who to listen to; which one of these can help me," always looking outside herself for the answers, the thing that would stabilize her. But she remained out of balance until she began looking for the answers within herself, for the fulcrum inside her . . . until she discovered that balance comes from within.

I wanted to write a whole chapter on balance, but as I mentioned, I wanted the book to have only eighteen chapters and a chapter on balance would have made nineteen. Where to discuss balance, I wondered. It's so important. Should I incorporate it in chapter seventeen on Love? No, that wasn't it. Perhaps I should just forget about having only eighteen chapters and make it a separate chapter? Then, as I was running yesterday, I discovered that it belongs here with child-mind . . . serendipity.

So, it's important to be flexible. To be willing to open up like a flower — gradually and fully. I don't know about you, but when I near the end of doing something all-consuming and passionate — like this book, I begin to lose focus, concentration, discipline. In my excitement about completing it, I begin to lose my center and my energy gets scattered and diffused. I become restless in the anticipation and thrill of finishing and the gnawing awareness that now is when I must pull it all together.

I had so much I still wanted to say, I didn't know how I would bring it all together in these last two chapters. Out of this restlessness, I found my answer . . . serendipity.

Exhausted yesterday, (the day after my friend and I went to the beach), I woke up wondering how will I ever write my chapter today. But not writing it was simply not an option.

So, I sat down to write what Natalie Goldberg calls "morning pages" — spontaneous, non-stop writing that is free association and uncontrolled by thought. In this way, I hoped to clear out the cobwebs in my mind. I began slowly at first, but as I proceeded to write, I worked through my fatigue, my restlessness, and almost Socratic-like, arrived without ever expecting to or knowing where I was going. As I wrote, I opened up petal by petal — like a flower. And then I ran — as my thought erupted in full bloom . . . serendipity.

And I knew what I had to write. Out of the chaos, came order. I excavated my exhaustion and restlessness as I wrote about my walk on the beach with my friend, and how I discovered the yin and the yang of child-mind; I was led to what I wanted and needed to write — to the core of it — where the truth, power and beauty of a thing always resides. I discovered the total integrity — the integrative reality of serendipity in child-mind.

And in discovering this, I discovered that I still have so much to learn, to discover and share and then to begin all over again and again and again. As T.S. Eliot tells us,

> *And the end of all our exploring*
> *Will be to arrive where we started*
> *And know the place for the first time.*

So it seems we are always as Rilke tells us, "So before all beginning." How wonderful! How serendipitous. . . .

About the Author

Madeleine Kay, life coach, teacher and communicator, is a former instructor at the University of Miami and other universities in the United States and abroad.

A lifelong student of metaphysics, she has an MA and has been helping people live more joyfully and abundantly for years with what she calls Eclectic Practical Therapy.

Founder of her own advertising, marketing and public relations agency of which she Creative Director, she is listed in *Who's Who in the South and Southwest.* As a freelance writer, she wrote social and political commentaries for the CBS affiliate in Miami, has traveled the world extensively and speaks four languages.

A native New Yorker now living in North Carolina and Florida, she is currently working on several other "Serendipity" books, as well as a short-story collection titled *How Will I Ever Get Over My Happy Childhood.*

Madeleine Kay is available for individual and small group sessions and coaching and to speak on *Living Serendipitously . . . Keeping the Wonder Alive.* She can be reached through:

Chrysalis Publishing
PO Box 675
Flat Rock, NC 28731
Tel. (828) 692-9840 / Fax (828) 698-8343
www.livingserendipitously.com

Notes

Kind acknowledgment is made for permission to reprint the following:

The lines from "i thank You God for most this amazing." Copyright 1950, © 1978, 1991 by the Trustees for the E.E. Cummings Trust. Copyright © 1979 by George James Firmage, from *Complete Poems: 1904-1962* by E.E. Cummings, edited by George J. Firmage. Used by permission of Liveright Publishing Corporation.

Excerpt from *The Seven Storey Mountain* by Thomas Merton, copyright 1948 by Harcourt, Inc. and renewed 1976 by the Trustees of The Merton Legacy Trust, reprinted by permission of Harcourt, Inc. and Sheldon Press.

Twenty lines from *A Return to Love* by Marianne Williamson. Copyright © 1992 by Marianne Williamson. Page 3. Reprinted by permission of HarperCollins Publishers, Inc. Portions reprinted from *A Course in Miracles*. Copyright © 1975 by Foundation for Inner Peace, Inc. All chapter openings are from *A Course in Miracles*.

Excerpt from *archy and mehitabel* by don marquis. Published by Doubleday, a division of Random House, Inc., reprinted by permission of the publisher.

Excerpts from *Letters To A Young Poet* by Rainer Maria Rilke, translated by M.D. Herter Norton. Copyright 1934, 1954 by W.W. Norton & Company, Inc., renewed © 1962, 1982 by M.D. Herter Norton. Used by permission of W.W. Norton & Company, Inc.

Excerpts from *The Power of Myth* by Joseph Campbell with Bill Moyers. Published by Doubleday, a division of Random House, Inc., reprinted by permission of the publisher.

Excerpt from *Hope for the Flowers* by Trina Paulus. Copyright © 1972 by Trina Paulus. Used with permission of Paulist Press. www.paulistpress.com

Various excerpts from *Siddhartha* by Hermann Hesse, translated by Hilda Rosner. Copyright © 1951 by New Directions Publishing Corp. Reprinted by permission of New Directions Publishing Corp. and Pollinger Limited.